Catholic Mom Challenge

Striving for Sainthood in Everyday Mom Life

By Sterling Jaquith

Dedication

I dedicate this book to our Blessed Mother. She guides everything I do and I love her with all my heart. Thank you for being my mama throughout this whole process.

This book would not be made possible without the hard work and brilliant ideas of
Matthew Kelly (www.dynamiccatholic.com)
Brian Johnson (www.brianjohnson.me) and
Ashley Woleban (www.betweenthelinens.com)

I am thankful for these people whom I consider my teachers.

Contents

Prologue

Chances are, you probably don't know me very well. I'm not a well-known Catholic speaker; my blog is still in its infancy, and I'm tucked away in Boise, Idaho where we don't have many large national events. This book is very personal, though, so I'd like you to consider me a friend. Friendship is not something that can be forced, so I asked myself, how could I genuinely connect with readers?

One of the best ways we form friendships is by sharing moments together: those times we're sitting and having a cup of coffee or standing at the edge of a park watching our children play. Those are the moments we open up about our real and true selves.

I want to be your friend, so I'm going to tell you a story about how God allowed me to stumble over myself so I would realize how much I needed Him in my life. It's also an embarrassing story; the kind I only tell my friends.

This story is about pride. I struggle a great deal with this sin. I think too highly of myself, and I'm often too judgmental of others. Don't get me wrong, I also struggle with deep, wallowing, self-loathing too. Inflated pride and self-loathing are merely different sides of the same coin – both are focused on oneself.

I'm working on curtailing these tendencies, and I'm a lot better than I used to be (through no power of my own). Having children has greatly humbled me. I also spend a great deal of time praying to Jesus, Mary, and the saints. Goodness knows I need all the help I can get!

My husband helps me battle my pride, too. I need his help every day. God gives us marriage so we can help each other get to Heaven. Most days, I am grateful for my husband's gentle nudging toward sainthood. If ever I squirm a little when he gently reminds me to let the air out of my own balloon, all he has to do is give me a small smile, and we both know why I instantly stop resisting and start praying!

I met my husband on eHarmony.[1] I was certain that I was too cool for him, and that we'd never get along. He was N-E-R-D-Y, and I don't mean the cute, hipster kind with black rimmed glasses and skinny jeans. He studied analytical chemistry, which is considered nerdy even by the other chemists.

I deigned to give him a chance because he was the only guy I had been matched with who said Jesus multiple times in his profile. I had been searching for a strong Christian man, but I was meeting a lot of "I go to church sometimes and I listen to Christian music" type guys, who didn't seem to have a real relationship with Christ. I decided to give this goofy chemist a chance.

God soothed my doubts along the way by revealing that this man was a huge dog lover. We found common ground in that and started corresponding a little. Then it turned into a lot. Suddenly I found myself getting quite attached to these words on a screen and the person they represented.

I started to wonder, "What if I'm wasting all this time writing to this chemist, and it turns out we have no chemistry together?" I reached out to my nerdy chemist and said, "Let's meet."

On our first date, he wore light blue denim shorts with white puffy tennis shoes. You know, a nod to the 80's. Not because he sported vintage fashion, but because he'd literally been wearing the same style of clothes since the 80's. His phone was in the front pocket of his white polo shirt like a sad Dilbert joke.

I smiled and fought the urge to run away. I had struggled to find any young man who loved Jesus (both online and in the person), so I couldn't simply throw this guy over because of some unfashionable clothes. I'm glad I stuck it out, though because we had a great first date.

It was full of laughs. It also had plenty of heated debates. I was a diehard Protestant and he was an uber-conservative Catholic so we had a lot to spar about. It turns out we liked our debates because we had four dates in four days. We were quite smitten with each other despite my constant claims that it would never work out because of our differing religious beliefs. He had enough hope for the both of us, and we continued to date.

On the fifth date, he graciously (and most impressively) made me a delicious salmon and asparagus dinner at his apartment. He opened up a bottle of wine and offered me some.

PAUSE.

I always pause for a moment before drinking alcohol. I'm a very lightweight drinker. In fact, I can handle just about two drinks. Sometimes not even that if the glasses are too big. I don't drink often, but whenever I do, I always make a plan in my head to only have two drinks followed by two glasses of water. I know this about myself, and I respect my boundaries.

So there we were. I was sitting on his awful, green, puffy microfiber couch in his poorly decorated apartment. I still thought I was way cooler than him. He took out these tiny wine glasses. They are the kind of wine glasses you would get in a wine tasting room. He told me he used to enjoy wine tasting when he lived in upstate New York. I thought this was adorable and I gladly accepted my tiny wine glass.

That was my problem right there.

I just assumed the glass was so tiny that I could probably have three glasses of wine and be just fine. I'm not even sure that this was a conscious thought, but there we were, cozy on his couch, watching a movie, and sipping wine. I was super nervous, and I wasn't paying attention to how many glasses I had.

Another thing you should know about me: I have a great game face when I'm drinking. I appear to be absolutely sober until two minutes before I jump down the rabbit hole and appear totally sloshed. There's almost no warning.

Now don't get the wrong idea about me. I rarely get drunk. Really, I'm a nice girl, and I hate feeling sick. But that night, while sitting on the couch, watching a movie with this man I didn't know would become my husband, it hit me. I realized I was about to throw up.

If you can't read stories about throwing up, bail right now.
If you can handle it, the story gets pretty funny.

I stood up, headed quickly, but not running so as to create alarm, to the bathroom. I walked through the door and I realized I wasn't going to make it to the toilet. It was an absurdly long bathroom with the toilet at the end. So I did the only thing I could think of...I put my hands up to catch my throw-up.

For future reference, your hands aren't really capable of holding liquid.

It basically hit my hands and then splattered back on my own face and shirt. I stumbled to the toilet by the second heave and threw up all over it. I'm not sure how I got so little actually inside the bowl.

I sat back with wide eyes. I just stared for a few minutes at the scene before me. Feeling much more sober and void of anything in my stomach, panic and adrenaline set in. What else was there to do? I started cleaning.

I grabbed toilet paper and started sopping up the mess. I wiped down the floor and the seat. I couldn't tell if two minutes or twelve minutes had passed by, but everything looked clean except the wad of toilet paper I'd put in the toilet.

Without thinking, I went to flush the toilet and it started filling up... and it didn't stop. It was going to overflow. I think my heart stopped in that moment and with no time to come up with a better plan, I reached in, grabbed all the toilet paper, which was now covered in yuck, and held it up above the toilet so the water flushed.

I was kneeling on the floor, holding a wet mess and I didn't know what to do. I looked over and noticed a small waste bin. I had no choice. I tossed the wet wad of toilet paper into the garbage.

At that point, I was just going through the motions. I'd stopped asking myself how awful this situation was. The floor and the toilet looked clean and the puke-soaked paper had been contained. I looked down at myself and saw that there was throw up all over me and in my hair. So I did what any reasonable girl would do in this situation. I decided to take a shower.

I hopped in the shower, thinking I'll never get another date with this man. I mean, this poor guy must think I'm a crazy person. I'd spent so much time thinking I was better than him and suddenly there I was, cleaning throw up out of my hair.

Turns out, he did think I was crazy.

I love my husband's version of this story. When you ask him, he'll tell you that when he heard me turn the shower on, he definitely thought I could be a psycho. He was actually worried that an insane person was in his apartment. He didn't have much time to dwell on this, though, because he remembered that he had done laundry that day and had taken all the towels out of his bathroom.

I cleaned up, turned the shower off and reached for a towel. But of course, there wasn't one. I heard a very gentle knock on the door. "Are you alright?" He asked.

I didn't say anything because really, what could I possibly say at that point? He quietly asked, "Do you need a towel?"

"Yes," I squeaked out in the most embarrassed, mousy voice adding, "And a t-shirt."

He opened the door just a crack and handed me a towel and one of his t-shirts. I came out of the bathroom, and my eyes were on the floor. I didn't know what to say. I was mortified. I have no words to explain that this never happens and I'm a nice girl. Previously a crazy night to me would be drinking a Coke *with caffeine* after 7 p.m.!

"I'm so sorry. I'm so sorry." That's all I managed to say. And with no more words, he just let me lay down on the ugly couch, which now mocked me with its cozy puffy pillows. This man, who would one day become my husband, didn't say anything about my wet hair soaking through the microfiber. Instead he gave me a blanket and said, "It's okay. Goodnight."

The next morning we talked for four hours. Amazingly, our relationship survived and grew even stronger. I think God allowed this embarrassing event to happen in order to knock me down a few pegs. I immediately stopped looking down my nose at my nerdy chemist and began pleading for him to give *me* another chance.

I stopped thinking of him as this nice, funny guy who I could never really be with. I started to see him for the strong, forgiving man who was able to see through my façade. He gave me a chance when I certainly didn't deserve one.

We often joke about that night. We say that God had to knock me down a few rungs so I could see what a good thing I had right in front of me. Ultimately, I would love and trust this man so much that he would lead me Catholicism.

This book is kind of like that night. I'll share a lot of my struggles and many of the reminders I've put in place to help me live a more Christ-centered life. Goodness knows we need to be constantly reminded that we're fighting for eternity and not for present comfort. The struggle can be hard day in and day out, but it's worth it.

We must set down our worldly addictions and our prideful preoccupations to turn to Jesus. That's what He asks of us. As we strive for sainthood, let us build a community and forge friendships with people who will help us along the way. Let's create a strong network of women who can help us see our own weaknesses and who will love us anyways

Few of us belong to a close-knit, Catholic community. Instead, we feel lonely in our suburban neighborhoods and have detached relationships on social media, which often lack depth. It may seem difficult to create genuine community, but we must set out to do this. We will have to be creative. We will have to be purposeful. Banding together in Catholic communion will help us in our mission to become saints.

Let's share our struggles and reveal our brokenness to each other. My hope is that through these friendships and with prayer, the grace of God will come and fill in the gaps.

Together, we can fight for what really matters. We can help each other see through the distractions and cling to our great Catholic faith. That's what the Catholic Mom Challenge is about. At first, you will challenge yourself, then you will make friends and challenge each other. We're talking about souls, so the stakes are high. The prize is eternity with our loving Father and each other.

Get ready to take the challenge. It will teach you to both fight for holiness and peace.

Introduction

*"The secret of happiness is to live moment by moment and
to thank God for all that He, in His goodness,
sends to us day after day."*
– St. Gianna Beretta Molla

The internet can be a fabulous place. How do I fix my dishwasher?
Find the manual online. What can I make for dinner with two cans of
tomato soup? There's a website to help you. I'm going to a wedding
and when it comes to hair, my A-game is a ponytail. Help! There's a
YouTube video for that.

When it comes to being a good mom, however, there's no simple
solution. Instead of finding no answer, we get a million answers, often
conflicting, about how we should go about this job of raising our
children and creating a strong family.

Should I homeschool my kids?

*How do I find time to be with my husband when I'm driving around to
soccer practice all the time?*

*They say "take care of yourself first," but that just seems selfish, and, even
when I have me time, I don't know what to do!*

Why is eating healthy food so expensive?

I'm drowning, and I don't even know where to start.

I have read dozens of parenting and marriage books looking for help,
searching for one guidebook to help me put everything in its place. But
of course, there could never be one perfect path for motherhood,
because we are all different mothers with different children, different
husbands, and completely different life situations.

The more I read, the more I found bits and pieces of things that I
thought made sense. Some of these sources weren't based on religion,
and some were religious but didn't seem to apply to motherhood. I

wanted so desperately to put all these good pieces of advice together in a way that I could wake up each day and know what to do.

With all this information, I didn't find the solution I was looking for.

Instead of implementing what I learned, I was paralyzed. I felt overwhelmed by all the exercises and tidbits of advice. I ended up sitting in my comfy, living room chair, staring at my daughters, and not doing anything. I felt like I was sleepwalking through my life. Not only was this dissatisfying, but my constant procrastination created more problems for me to face in the future.

One day, I snapped. It wasn't the "angry, losing your mind, emotional, break-down" kind of snap. It was more like a bucket of cold water being thrown on my face.

Sterling, you're an adult. You wake up each day and you get to choose what to do. Even when God throws you curve balls, you always get to choose how you react. You can be intentional about your day or you can choose to remain ignorant and stagnant.

I knew there were simple fixes to my problems. They weren't going to be easy, but they were simple. I realized that what I needed was something physical I could turn to for a quick snapshot of what was important to me, tips for successfully tackling those important things and ways to overcome common obstacles that would get in my way. I put a time limit on combing through all the books I had read, and I pulled out the themes and simple tips I felt could help me live a more intentional, Christ-centered life.

I made a little booklet, which was really a Word document that I printed out and stapled. I called it my Catholic Mom Manifesto. And you know what? It really worked. When my kids lost their minds, when my marriage was struggling, and when my health was failing, I would pull out this book and it was like an anchor. Right there on every page was my commitment to living a Christ-centered life.

This little booklet was really pointing me back to Him.

After I made this system for myself, it helped give me focus and peace. The more peace I experienced, the more I wanted to share it with other women. I thought, what if I created a system to help moms craft their own guidebook, their very own Map to Being a Great Mom? Everyone's map would look different. It works like a GPS system – when we take detours from the best path, we have to recalculate our route to continue our journey.

The system has to be flexible because our lives are always changing.

That is what I've created for you. And really, to be honest, I created it for me, because I needed something to anchor me to what is really important - to what really matters - instead of drifting in and out of memes and blogs and perfect Instagram photos.

This is what the Catholic Mom Challenge is all about.

It should be no surprise the whole thing is built on a foundation of Christ. We all know we should be living every day walking with Jesus, but we feel stymied. Living a Catholic life can seem confusing and as out of reach as the scene in a beautiful painting on your wall. You know you want to go there but you keep saying, "Someday when things are less crazy."

So ladies, let's get real. I'm going to give you a system to help identify what your priorities are and to tackle them. I mean, to really *crush* them. Grab life by the shoulders and say, "I can do this!"

It's going to be hard.

It's going to be messy sometimes.

You're going to want to give up and hide under the covers and binge-watch Downton Abbey on your phone while eating a bag of chips and ignoring your kids. Don't worry, I'm going to let you know what to do after this happens, too.

This system can change you. It can forge you into the person you want to be. Ultimately, we're trying to forge you into the person God wants you to be. He knows everything about you, including what would make you feel the deepest fulfillment in this life. He also knows exactly what you need in order to spend eternity with Him.

This is a framework that you fill in with your own personal details, so it doesn't matter if you have one little baby or twelve kids. It doesn't matter if you have a military husband who is gone all the time or a dad who works from home (and is always in your space.) It doesn't matter if you can't eat dairy or have a child with a disability. It doesn't matter if you are struggling to pay for private school or if you have chosen to homeschool your kids.

This system works for everyone because it will teach you to always be refining what works for you. It's about treating life as one big experiment where we run tests, keep what works, and toss what doesn't. It's always evolving to meet your needs.

This system will put you in charge of your own life.

I know this because it radically changed my life. I went from being an apathetically, unhealthy 205 pounds; always forgetting or not being able to pay my bills; sad, lonely, disorganized (oh the piles!); and wanting to scream at my kids or ignore them to prioritizing my health, sticking to a budget, building community, getting organized, and being a mom who actually knows how to enjoy her children.

Do I still mess it up? Of course! But now, when I do, I go straight back to the system and get on track quickly so my bad choices don't derail me for as long.

Most of us have a deep longing in our hearts. This is our desire for God, to love Him and to be like Jesus.

Another way to say this is to say that we should all be striving to be saints. Our whole lives should be working up to sainthood, so that when we get to Heaven, Jesus will say, "Well done, my good and faithful servant." We do this, not for the accolades, but because the deepest longing in our soul is to be like God because we were made in His image.

The best path to sainthood and to becoming our most Holy selves is to strive to be the "best-version-of-ourselves". This is a phrase coined by Matthew Kelly who says, "Holiness doesn't dampen our emotions; it elevates them. Those who respond to God's call to holiness are the most joyful people in history. They have a richer, more abundant experience of life, and they love more deeply than most people can ever imagine. They enjoy life, all of life."

I want to live that kind of life, to be that kind of person.

I used to say to myself that I would do something really hard, if only Jesus appeared and asked. If God would send down an angel and tell me to do *anything*, then, of course, I'd throw my whole self into it without question. But this is a rare gift directly bestowed on only a few people on this earth. The rest of us must continue to live our lives without receiving divine memos on what to do.

It's the *not knowing* that's hard. It's the constant questioning.

What am I supposed to do?

Who should get my time and my effort?

What's really important in life, and how do I protect it?

The Catholic Mom Challenge is going to help you figure this out. We'll dive into seven main areas of your life: spirituality, motherhood, marriage, health, finances, homemaking and rest. It's not so much a vertical list as it is a circle. They all work together. They are moving parts that touch each other.

So if you're ready to take charge of your life, if you're ready to leave the doubt and worry behind, turn the page, and let's get started!

How To Use This Book

This book is a tool. You can read it from front to back before diving into the exercises. Alternatively, you can jump straight to The Catholic Mom Challenge System, and start filling out the worksheets that accompany this book. Here is an overview of the three main sections:

The Great Circle of Life

Here you will find an overview of the seven life facets of your life covered in The Catholic Mom Challenge system. I share my own struggles and successes, as well as pose questions you can ask yourself to help you craft your Catholic Mom Manifesto.

The Catholic Mom Challenge System

Here you will learn how to use the system, create a Life Plan and go through the Annual Planning process. You will use all this information to create your own Catholic Mom Manifesto; a small booklet that you will keep with you to help live a Christ-centered life. Finally, you'll create a plan each week to help you stay focused.

What to do When *Life* Happens

Here I will give you the tools you'll need to navigate bumps in the road, overcome obstacles that come your way, and to bounce back from failure if you get seriously derailed.

Even if you skip the first section of the book because you're eager to start filling out worksheets, (I often have this impulse myself,) I suggest you read the third section before creating your Catholic Mom Manifesto. This section has a lot of wisdom and can help you make more realistic plans. More than anything, I want to help you live a more peaceful and intentional life. Thank you for reading this book and for taking on The Catholic Mom Challenge!

Part One:

The Great Circle of Life

The Great Circle of Life

Cue the Lion King Music

"You must ask God to give you power to fight against the sin of pride which is your greatest enemy – the root of all that is evil, and the failure of all that is good. For God resists the proud."
– St. Vincent de Paul

Lay your pride down as you pick up this book. Let your heart be open to what God has to say to you. I will challenge you to loosen your grip on what the world tells you to love. Instead, I will encourage you to turn your heart toward Jesus. This is always scary.

It has been whispered in your ear that the joys here on earth are better than those in Heaven, or worse, that Heaven may not even exist. It's the devil who whispers those lies.

When you hear the evil one's voice as you are reading this book, ask God to give you the grace to fight against the sin of pride. For God is the Truth, the Life, and the Way.

We are going to focus on seven areas of your life: spirituality, marriage, motherhood, health, finances, homemaking, and rest. We have often heard these different areas of our lives listed out as a vertical list of priorities.

How many times have you read that you should first prioritize God, then your spouse, then children? I think this idea is used so often because it's easy to focus on the loudest challenges in front of us, often the children. We let our quieter relationships, with God and our husbands, slip into the background.

While I agree that focusing on our children to the detriment of our spirituality or our marriage is dangerous, I don't think our priorities can be fixed in place every moment of our lives. Sometimes the children *are* more important. When your daughter is in the NICU, your housekeeping schedule should not be a top priority. Sometimes our financial situation has gotten so out of control that it deserves to be our main focus.

These seven areas of our life fit together like a circle, each touching the other. They are all related. They move in and out of being the most important thing in the moment, for the day, and for a season. We are going to call each of these seven life areas "facets."

While each facet of your life is very different, they all represent part of who you are. Like a beautiful diamond, each facet makes up part of your unique identity. We're going to go through and see which facets have become dull; they need to be shined so they can sparkle again.

This will be a continual process, we will be constantly asking ourselves, "Which area of my life needs improvement?"

These facets of our life make up a circle. By thinking of them this way, instead of a rigid list, it allows us to continually be shifting our focus. We cannot always be praying or parenting. And yet, when we focus and build up one area of our life, it benefits the other areas. When one part of the circle stretches, it forces the other parts to grow.

We must make small improvements in each of these seven facets and constantly evaluate which one needs our attention at the moment.

For example, it's hard to work on your finances if your marriage is a mess and you and your husband are arguing all the time. It's difficult to be a great parent if your health is failing. You shouldn't retreat to the kitchen to make food for seven hours and ignore your children. It is all a balance.

We must identify baby steps and push ourselves to make more good choices and fewer bad choices. Mama, you're smart. You know what you need to do. You may feel overwhelmed, but right now, you could easily list three things to *start* doing and three things to *stop* doing that would make your life better.

When I soothe my stressful day with a $5 peppermint mocha, I know I'm making a bad choice. It's not good for my health, my finances, or my spirituality, because I should be leaning on Jesus instead of sweet, sugary coffee. This isn't universally a bad choice. You may enjoy the same coffee with a friend on a bright, sunny Saturday and have money in your budget for the coffee and be in a healthy place so you can handle a sugary treat.

Many parts of the Catholic Mom Challenge will be relative to your own life situation. Some parts, like daily prayer, will be non-negotiable tasks every Catholic woman should undertake.

Most of us are aware of our bad habits, and we know which good habits we should have instead. I think the real challenge is identifying the bad habits we need to lose, and prioritizing which new habits to instill. We can make a long list, but we don't know where to start. Even if we do manage to start, we're afraid we'll stop and go back to our old habits. The Catholic Mom Challenge system can help you get clarity.

Rest assured, this system did not arrive on these pages without a lot of refining. I crashed and burned through years of confusion about my faith, an awkward marriage, chaotic motherhood, broken finances, depleted health, very little rest and little to no homemaking skills. I learned just how much I needed Jesus, and a little booklet, to survive it all.

Not only do I survive it all now, but I do so with more hope, peace, and intentionality than I have ever experienced. I still have bad days and tough seasons but I bounce back from them so much faster. I spend a lot less time wallowing and, instead, I give thanks to God and move forward.

This book is about moving forward, taking baby steps, and striving for sainthood. Let's start with the most important facet of our life: our spirituality.

Chapter One:
Spirituality

"God gives each one of us sufficient grace ever to know
His holy will, and to do it fully."
– St. Ignatius of Loyola

I've introduced the idea that these 7 facets of our life make up a circle. I'd like, however, to revise that visual and suggest that six facets make up a circle, and if you turn it over, the entire back of the circle says SPIRITUALITY. Every single part of our life should be based on the foundation of our faith.

Later, you'll see in the Catholic Mom Challenge System that we are always evaluating what needs our attention and shifting around our daily and weekly priorities. However, the one constant we're working on is our faith. No matter what season we're in, being faithful to God will always be the foundation of our life from which we will tackle everything else.

I've learned a great deal about the faith since I converted to Catholicism. This book assumes you have a basic understanding of our faith. If you're Catholic but you don't know much about our wonderful religion, I suggest you go to my website and read some of the Catholic 101 books I list there. Rather than focus on the basics, I'm going to propose five actions that will greatly deepen your faith life:

- Make God your best friend (even though you can't see him);
- Consecrate yourself to Jesus through Mary;
- Have a strong prayer life;
- Work hard;
- Embrace suffering.

While the list above is simple, it can seem overwhelming to fit them into your daily life. Let's break down each one and then we'll talk about how to slowly introduce these practices into your life.

Make God Your Best Friend

"Lord, I am Yours, and I must belong to no one but You.
My soul is Yours, and must live only by You. My will is
Yours, and must love only for You. I must love You as my
first cause, since I am from You. I must love You as my
end and rest, since I am for You. I must love You more
than my own being, since my being subsists by You. I
must love You more than myself, since I am all Yours and
all in You. Amen."
–St. Francis de Sales

It can be difficult to make God (a seemingly formless, silent, ethereal Being,) more important to you than your husband, your children, or your friends. We intellectually know He *is* more important, but our feelings don't always tell the same story.

When I don't feel warm and fuzzy about Christ, it doesn't mean I have stopped loving Him or that He has stopped loving me. My love for Him is a choice and a commitment. I love Him out of my own free will, whether I have warm feelings or I feel nothing at all. As Fr. John Riccardo says often, "Love begins when the feelings are gone."[2] As with our other friendships, sometimes we can feel grumpy with God. We don't always feel His presence and so we can instead feel abandoned. Even though scripture tells us that God will never leave us, when we experience spiritual dryness, we still feel all alone.

When I first became a Christian, I was overwhelmed by feelings of love, warmth, and comfort. It was like being wrapped up in the softest security blanket. It made me feel blissfully happy to simply walk down the street because I had this new friend who loved me more than I could even imagine. It was as if I was surrounded by a mist of joy everywhere I went. It can be easy to think this is how being a Christian should feel all the time.

As many Christians will tell you, those feelings can fade. When the honeymoon period has worn off, we are left to make a choice. Will we continue to love and serve the Lord without the good feelings? Or, will we treat our faith like a fad and move on to the next thing that brings us temporary happiness? St. Teresa of Avila captures this sentiment beautifully.

> *"They deceive themselves who believe that union with*
> *God consists in ecstasies or raptures, and in the*
> *enjoyment of Him. For it consists in nothing except the*
> *surrender and subjection of our will - with our thoughts,*
> *words, and actions - to the will of God."*
> *- St. Teresa of Avila*

God is not a vending machine. Our friends don't like to be used and neither does God. Most of us are more generous and kind to our friends than we are to Jesus. We must seek to form a relationship with Him, because God created us to know Him, love Him and serve Him. We don't send up our prayers so we can receive warm feelings and good fortune. We love Him because He created us to love Him. Even if we're living in the middle of YEARS of spiritual dryness, we will only find fulfillment by loving and serving Him.

It's hard to prioritize our spiritual life when we can't always *feel* grace. When you work out, you sweat. When you eat healthy food, there's some evidence of your effort. When you spend twenty minutes reading to your children, you might have an internal sense of "job well done!"

When we make the time to pray, go to Adoration, go to Confession, attend a daily Mass, or read our Bibles, sometimes we feel nothing. Or worse, sometimes we're interrupted by our children (or life in general), and our spiritual experience is unpleasant and difficult.

We are surely given grace in our spiritual efforts, but we can't always feel that this has occurred. It's easy to doubt that our time given to God really matters. If I asked you, "Do you think your time in daily Mass is valuable?" You'd probably say, "Yes, of course, God honors our time," and you'd mean it. But when your kids won't put on their jackets and they say, "Mooooom, I don't want to go to daily Mass," and you notice it's raining outside, it can be easy to think it doesn't *really* matter. We could just stay home.

I am not saying you need to get your kids dressed for daily Mass every day. God bless you if you manage to do that, and I know some amazing Catholic moms who do! There are many seasons of life, and that's why our great Catholic church has given us so many different ways of living out our faith. In my current phase of life, I try to go to daily Mass every Wednesday. Sometimes I get inspired to go an extra day, and some weeks Wednesday mass slips by.

The system is not about creating strict routines and sticking to them at the sake of harming the family. Rather, the point is that we need to examine our motivations. If I'm pregnant and can't leave the couch crippled by morning sickness, I don't worry about going to daily Mass. Just like a good friend, God understands when we are not at our best.

There are, however, times when I want to go to daily Mass, I am perfectly capable of going, and I even feel the nudge of the Holy Spirit saying, "Today is a good day to go." I *still* decide to take the path of least resistance and hang out at home in my jammies and, for me, that's a bad choice. I'm being selfish, and I'm not being a good friend to the Lord anymore.

I'm picking daily Mass as an example here, but this is true about all the important Catholic pillars (prayer, Mass, Confession, Adoration and Bible reading.) We need to make our relationship with God our highest priority because that effort is going to give us the strength to tackle the remaining facets of our life.

God created us to be divinized – to be filled with His divine life. This is why, even when you're connecting with your husband and on great terms with your children, there is still a longing in your heart. There is always a hole inside of you that you long to fill. If you've stopped nurturing your faith, it can be easy to think that maybe you need a hobby or some alone time. While those things may be true, our deepest desire is and always will be for the Lord.

An important part of the Catholic Mom Challenge is to always make God your center. He is your best friend and your most important relationship. You must connect with Him every day, even if all you can manage is ten minutes of prayer time. But you must be intentional about this relationship if you want it to grow. You cannot go days without spending time with Jesus. You cannot leave Him in the background.

You also can't go and see Him begrudgingly with a heart full of bitterness. Well, you can of course, but that's not what He wants from you. If you're in a bad place, if you feel covered by darkness, it's okay to go to the Lord and tell Him you're in a bad place. There are many times I sit in Adoration and tell Him that I feel frustrated. I feel empty and selfish. But I go and give Him my whole and honest self because I love Him.

I give Him my time obediently because He has asked me to, even if I don't feel any grace. I make time because my faith is my top priority. I know that it strengthens the other six facets of my life.

I am a long way from having a perfect relationship with our Lord. There are times when I feel bitter and I want to hold back. I want to keep my broken sex life in a dark corner away from God. I want to stuff my feelings of unworthiness with nachos after my children have gone to bed instead of taking it to prayer. I want to be strong and solve all the problems of my extended family by myself because God isn't doing what I asked of Him.

These are normal thoughts. They are toxic but they are normal. This quote is in my Catholic Mom Manifesto and I read it often to remind myself that by holding back from God, I'm only hurting myself.

"Few souls understand what God would effect in them if they should give themselves entirely into his hands and allow his grace to act." - St. Ignatius of Loyola[3]

Accept and embrace that God needs to be the most important relationship in your life. You're going to find that improving your relationship with Him will improve all the other areas of your life. I'd like to say you will feel good about the changes, but the truth is, sometimes when we draw closer to God, the resulting changes may be painful.

God made us to know Him, to love Him and to serve Him. I repeat this phrase because it's something I teach my children. We repeat this often in our household. The more I say it to them, the more I realize how many adults Catholics need to hear it too.

God made us to know Him, to love Him and to serve Him. This is a fantastic positive affirmation to say to yourself throughout the day. We must make this the center of our lives. It's a challenging thing to do because God can be so quiet. We can get caught up in grocery runs, Netflix marathons, soccer practice, and even church bake sales and never sit down to talk with our Father.

God wants to be your best friend. He wants you to tell Him everything. This is one of my favorite quotes from St. Faustina's diary, where she relays a conversation she had with Jesus:

> "My daughter...why do you not tell me about everything that concerns you, even the smallest details? Tell Me about everything, and know that this will give Me great joy. I answered, But You know about everything, Lord." And Jesus replied to me, "Yes I do know; but you should not excuse yourself with the fact that I know, but with childlike simplicity talk to Me about everything, for my ears and heart are inclined towards you, and your words are dear to Me.(2; 921)" --St. Faustina, Divine Mercy in my Soul[4]

Create a personal relationship with God. Nurture it. Prioritize it. In Appendix A, there are some questions to consider about your spirituality. I purposely didn't put them here because these questions need to be answered after prayer time and discernment. They should not be rushed.

The Protestants do a great job of voicing the importance of having a personal relationship with Jesus Christ. Sometimes Catholics feel uncomfortable even saying that phrase. If you feel that you don't know what having a real relationship with Christ looks like, I suggest you make this your first step as part of your commitment to growing in your faith. A commitment to understanding what it means to make Jesus your friend should be a top priority for everyone.

Consecrate Yourself To Mary

"Have you strayed from the path leading to heaven? Then call on Mary, for her name means 'Star of the Sea, the North Star which guides the ships of our souls during the voyage of this life,' and she will guide you to the harbor of eternal salvation."
St. Louis de Montfort, *The Secret of the Rosary*[5]

If you've ever seen me speak at a conference or listened to my podcast *Coffee & Pearls*, you know that I am on a mission to get every single person on the planet to consecrate herself to Jesus through Mary. I honestly believe this is what we need to do if we want to heal the many wounds of humankind. I doubt I'll see this goal accomplished in my lifetime, but I am certain that with every person who goes through this consecration process, we will be one step closer to living in a more peaceful world.

I have yet to meet a person who has gone through consecration who doesn't consider it to be a significant life-changing event. It is impossible to ignore how very changed one is by the process. Even if you dedicate your whole life to Mary only to fall off the wagon and forget about her, she is still there with you. She will always watch over you and whisper her truth and love into your heart.

Don't expect life to be all sunshine and roses after your consecration. You may still experience great darkness. Saint Theresa of Calcutta had a deep devotion to Mary after her consecration but still had many years of spiritual dryness. We will each be tested in unique ways. We will each carry a different cross. The path of consecration is not one of ease, but rather of peace. Even in the darkness, you can have peace and hope by walking with Jesus and His beloved mother.

Most of us will experience bouts of spiritual dryness in our lifetime. This first happened to me right after I converted to Catholicism. After leaving Protestantism, I expected the Catholic Church to throw me a big party. Instead, I was met with coldness from my new parish, and I felt great darkness in my previously vibrant spiritual life. Spiritual dryness can be extremely confusing and painful. I don't think we discuss this topic enough, and when people encounter it, they feel as if they're the only ones experiencing this darkness.

When we are in spiritual dryness, we are never really alone; God never leaves us. One of the great gifts of our Catholic faith is the communion of saints. We have access to thousands of men and women who lived through spiritual dryness and are eager to pray for us in our own times of darkness.

I have yet to read about a saint who didn't go through periods of doubt and spiritual dryness. These stories can help you to remain strong in your faith even when you feel alone and abandoned by God. I promise that He has not abandoned you. He loves you very much and He does have a plan for you. By getting to know our Blessed Mother, you will come to understand the heart of Jesus more fully.

Before I went through consecration, I was somewhat indifferent about Mary. You might have guessed that, as a former Protestant, I had strong feelings against Mary, but I never did. She was just kind of there – neither good nor bad. It was in the fall of 2014 that I began hearing stories of women who had gone through consecration and claimed it had changed their lives. At the time, I didn't really understand what consecration was about, but their testimonies and the great joy they expressed were certainly a compelling reason to give it a try.

I went through the *33 Days To Morning Glory* program written by Fr. Michael Gaitley[6]. I did this in a small group; we met in the living room of someone's house. It was a messy and imperfect group study, but when you have little kids, you have to settle for that sometimes. God still meets us when we're surrounded by toddler toys and bouncing babies.

My husband and I went through the program together. We usually read different spiritual books or go through Bible study programs at separate times. For some reason, though, we chose to do this one together, and it was one of the best things we've ever done for our marriage. We didn't realize it was going to be a big deal, but it really did change us. I will always consider this one of the biggest blessings of my life.

Before this program, I used to worry all the time. I have a lot of people in my family who need help; either they struggle with their health or their finances, or they do not believe in Jesus. My heart was always heavy with worry for each of them. I would lie in bed at night thinking, "Lord, how can I take care of them all?"

After my consecration, I gave my entire family to Mary. This is a process described in Gaitley's book. You entrust your loved ones to Mary and then you stop worrying about them. It sounded too good to be true, and I'm not sure I believed it would really happen for me. That's the thing about Mary, though. She wants to take care of everyone in your life and she brings about impossible things through Christ.

For many months after my consecration, a great peace came over me. I felt a wonderful freedom in not having to worry about my family. Like becoming a Christian for the first time, that warmth and quiet bliss surrounded me wherever I went. I would take a deep sigh and smile, knowing that Mary was going to take care of my family.

There are times when I am not as close to Mary as I would like. Perhaps I forget to pray my consecration prayer or I let a few days slip without praying my rosary. As soon as Mary fades into the background, my worry creeps back in. I have to stop my mind from spinning on the anxious-wheel and immediately turn back toward her. This system is going to help you find those guides to help you get back on track when you lose your way.

Mary is a guide that everyone needs.

She is everyone's mother. You cannot out-love her. I know that my family will still go through suffering, but I have a peace about it. I trust that she is watching out for them and asking her Son to care for my family. Even now, I'm not sure what all that entails, but I trust her.

If you want to grow in spirituality and you have not gone through Marian consecration, I highly suggest you consider it. Don't take it lightly. You are basically giving complete control of your whole life to our Blessed Mother. If you do feel called to this right now in your life, I recommend the 33 Days program. If you want something more intense or academic, you can pick one of the older, more involved programs like *True Devotion* by Louis De Montfort[7].

I go through this retreat every year and renew my consecration vows on November 21st. I say my vows every day but I do the formal process each year because it really is that important and has been such a key to my own peace and contentment in life. One of my favorite prayers from the program really sums up what I want for my life.

> *"Mary, I want to be a saint. I know that you also want me to be a saint and that it's your God-given mission to form me into one. So, Mary, at this moment, on this day, I freely choose to give you my full permission to do your work in me, with your Spouse, the Holy Spirit."*
>
> - *Fr. Michael Gaitley, 33 Days to Morning Glory*[8]

Have a Strong Prayer Life

We all know we need to pray. This isn't new information and yet somehow, we manage to *not* pray all the time. We can let hours, days and even weeks go by when we get so wrapped up in our own thoughts and conversations that we forget to pray. I am consistently guilty of this!

Despite the fruits of my prayer life, I still manage to forget to pray. Worse, I often let my prayer life fall by the wayside just when my life is starting to crumble. You'd think in times of crisis, I would naturally turn to prayer!

Humans are naturally rebellious. We squirm at being told what to do. We want to break out of our parent's homes and be our own people. We think we want to be free, but freedom doesn't actually mean, "Do whatever you want." That is not true freedom. Instead, doing whatever you feel like doing will lead you into a dark prison of your own making.

When things aren't going well, I have this tendency to want to "be free" from God as if separating myself from the Creator of the world will make things better somehow.

I struggle to put into words what I feel emotionally when things around me are falling apart. The deeply dark and ugly times are hard to describe: when I miscarried my babies, when my marriage was rocky, and when I can't seem to control my emotional eating. My heart feels like it is holding bitterness, disappointment, anger, entitlement and shame all swirled together. Sin festers because part of me is angry with God and somewhere along the way, I stop trusting Him.

I have lived through darkness many times in my life. I know how it feels to live a life without God, without prayer. I did this for years before I became a Christian. Since then, I have also found myself turned away from God out of bitterness and anger. In these times my prayer life has dwindled to nothing.

This life is hard. We will have many trials before we are called home to Heaven. Even when living deeply faithful lives, many of us go through periods when we stop praying. I want to call out daily prayer as something that is absolutely crucial for Catholics. We have to maintain a strong prayer life as we strive for sainthood.

Here is a visual I like to keep in my mind to help me maintain my prayer life.

Imagine there is a candle inside of your heart. God is the candle and when you pray, He breathes air into your heart so the candle shines brightly. His light allows you to see His love for you, to see His fingerprints on your life even in difficult situations. When you stop praying, it's as if the air slowly gets sucked out of the room and your candle fades. The fire dies down and the light gets suffocated. God never leaves you but when you live without prayer, the darkness sets in.

Don't let this happen to you. Whenever you find yourself calling out, "God where are you? Why have you left me?" I want you to immediately check in with yourself about your prayer time. Have you let it slip by? Has your candle gone out?

The good news is prayer is free and easy; you can do it anytime and anywhere! Stop right now and say a quick thirty-second prayer to our Lord. It doesn't have to be beautiful. It doesn't have to have complete sentences. If you can't think of anything, say an Our Father. If you're too angry with God to manage those words, simply cry out, "Jesus!"

There is real power in the name of Jesus. Sometimes that's the only word I can manage while tears stream down my face because the hurts I've endured are so painful. I'm not asking you to be strong, I'm asking you to be faithful.

There are times still when I sink into the darkness, but I try to think of that candle and I start to pray. I know that praying is the way out of the blackness. Darkness cannot exist where there is light. God is light. Bring Him back into your life.

There are many different forms of prayer and ways to pray. Pick one that works for you and just do it. Change it often if you need to keep your prayer life fresh. Most of all, be obedient and pray every single day. Treat God like your best friend. He wants you to tell Him everything.

Get To Work

*"I can't do big things. But I want all I do, even the
smallest thing, to be for the greater glory of God."*
– St. Dominic Savio

You are going to die. You are going to work and suffer for your entire life, and then you are going to die. If that makes you uncomfortable, it should. Our bodies will die, and our time here on Earth is limited. It is one thing I can guarantee. What happens afterward is up to you.

Before you accuse me of being a downer, realize that we all need to hear the truth even if we don't like it. My generation doesn't talk much about death. We live for the short-term. We pretend as if science and medicine will keep advancing, and we're all going to live to one hundred. That seems so far away, we don't concern ourselves with death much.

We are too focused on what's happening around us. We are surrounded by so much noise and screen time that we don't sit in silence anymore. We don't think about death. We don't ask ourselves what we want to accomplish in our own lifetime. I am suggesting that we make sainthood our aim. The great work that we have to do here on earth is to become saints.

We do this by keeping our eyes fixed on the prize. In order to do this, we have to drown out the many distractions the world will throw at us. We must be diligent in fighting for eternity. Consider the advice given by St. Anselm:

> "If you would be quite sure of your salvation, strive to be among the fewest of the few. Do not follow the majority of mankind, but follow those who renounce the world and never relax their efforts day or night so that they may attain everlasting blessedness." -St. Anselm, Doctor of the Church[9]

Even though thinking about death seems morbid and uncomfortable, it's very important. God does not want us to live in fear but we must be aware that our time on Earth is fleeting. It is not that we should be afraid of our mortality, but rather know that because our time is short, we have a great work to do while we are alive. We must understand that we have eternal souls that are bound for either Heaven or Hell.

God has given each of us a choice. We can choose to love and follow Him, or we can choose to ignore Him. The way you live your life is your answer to this choice. If you are sleepwalking through your own life, it's likely you're making the wrong choice without even realizing it. We all hope that God is loving and forgiving, and He is, but that doesn't mean we get a free pass to Heaven simply because we call ourselves Catholic. I think too many of us live a life of selfishness and greed and are banking on our Sunday Mass attendance to meet the requirements of salvation.

Salvation must be our ultimate goal, and we cannot let anything get in the way of this. We must also do our best to lead all the people around us to salvation! The stakes are eternity with God or eternity without Him.

Striving for sainthood is no picnic. We're not going to hole up in our homes, read the Bible, and live an easy, care-free life. That's not what God wants from most of us.

God created us for work. If I told you that you could live for free on a sandy beach somewhere and spend your days lounging in a hammock sipping your favorite drink and doing your favorite pastime, you'd probably say, "Sign me up!" I think most of us would enjoy that life for a week or two. But eventually you would become unhappy. You would be bored, unfulfilled, and a bit confused.

"Surely I should be happy hanging out in paradise, right?"

You wouldn't be.

We were not made for leisure alone. We could never be happy if we had no work to do. In Anthony DeStefano's book *Travel Guide To Heaven*[10], he explains the importance of work and that we will have work to do even once we get to Heaven:

> "Working in Heaven will be more satisfying and exciting than anything we've ever done in this life. In fact, it will be a key

part of what makes us happy. First, we have to understand that work is not a human invention. It's from God. Even if we had all the money in the world, we'd still need to engage in some form of labor because that need has been programmed in us by our Creator."

As soon as I read this, it really resonated with me. It also helped me to calm down a little bit because I realized, that up until this point, I had been living my life trying to get from one leisure activity to the next, viewing the work in between as a necessary chore.

I wanted to be comfortable. I wanted to do the least amount of work possible until I could relax again. The idea of working hard stressed me out. I would do it quickly so I could be done, or I would try to avoid it altogether. This tendency didn't stop when I became a mother; it just highlighted it. Suddenly, I was the one who had to do all the dishes and vacuum the floors. If I didn't make dinner, there were seriously loud consequences. I considered these many mundane tasks to be drudgery and I was starting to hate my own life filled with work.

I was blind to the fact that God had called me to motherhood, and this was the work He was asking me to do. Once I embraced that, I started to view all my activities differently. Don't get me wrong; this didn't happen overnight. I didn't suddenly hear angels singing and jump out of bed cheerily each morning, looking forward to doing the dishes. I had to read this message in books and blog articles over a few years before I finally gave it a real try.

I opened my heart up to the idea that I could serve God, yes, with a cheerful attitude by doing these mundane, everyday tasks. At first I was terrible at it. I would begin the day thanking Jesus for being alive, and I would start tackling my motherhood to-do list. Sometimes I wouldn't even make it until 9 a.m. before feeling frustrated with my children and fed up at having to clean sticky banana off the floor, because my ungrateful border collie (who eats almost anything) won't eat bananas!

In all of these tiny moments, I learned to pay attention to my soul. I learned how to sense when my soul was turned toward God, and I could sense when I had it turned away. The more I worked on thinking of myself turning toward God or turning away, the easier it became to right my attitude. I had been practicing this idea for a little over six months when I discovered an album on Amazon Prime Music called "25 Sunday School Songs Kids Love to Sing."[11] And on this album, there is a song called "Whisper a Prayer." Here are the lyrics:

> *Whisper a prayer in the morning,*
> *Whisper a prayer at noon;*
> *Whisper a prayer in the ev'ning,*
> *To keep your heart in tune.*
>
> *God answers prayer in the morning,*
> *God answers prayer at noon;*
> *God answers prayer in the ev'ning,*
> *To keep your heart in tune.*
>
> *Jesus may come in the morning,*
> *Jesus may come at noon;*
> *Jesus may come in the ev'ning,*
> *So keep your heart in tune.*

This was precisely what I had been trying to put words too! When I was younger I used to play the violin. Every time you take your violin out of the case, you have to check it to see if it's still in tune. So it made perfect sense to me that you would tune your heart like you would tune an instrument.

How beautiful would this world be if we all paused for a moment and thought of Jesus before using our hearts? Even when our hearts are only slightly tuned into the world instead of Christ, we can use them poorly and create so much harm. We can hurt those around us and ourselves.

I enjoy this little song because it reminds me that Jesus may come at any time. I pray deeply that when He comes, my heart is in tune with Him. I try to do this all throughout the day when I'm speaking with my husband and children. I try to stamp out the bitterness in my heart when I'm doing something God asks me to do that I don't feel like doing. God doesn't send angels to tell us to clean our bathroom. He puts people and responsibilities in our path to be good stewards of.

When I serve Him with joy, I find true peace, even in the mundane things, and I feel that my heart is in tune. The more I practice tuning into the Lord, the more I am able to tell when my heart is out of tune, and I seek to fix it quickly.

I realize now that work is necessary. God created us to work. If I didn't have any work at all, I'd be frustrated. The work God created us for is unique to each us. Once I embraced this and realized I was going to work for the rest of my life, it gave me peace. I felt so much calmer.

I no longer feel like I'm trying to escape my responsibilities. I'm no longer wishing for my carefree college days. I try to find purpose in the work that I do. When I'm embracing the work God intended me for, my soul is peaceful and content. It's not easy and plenty of things still frustrate me (I do have three young children.)

The difference is, now I know how to turn back toward God. I thank Him for what He has asked me to do, and I get to work!

If you feel trapped in your own life; if you feel like the drudgery of motherhood is weighing you down; if you cry at the idea that the laundry will never stop, the kids will always be pulling on you, and the bills will never be paid; and you'll always be thirty pounds overweight, take a deep breath.

I used to feel like that. I used to wonder why God would give me talents and then turn me into a mother of many small children, leaving those talents aside to do a job I was terrible at.

I see my life differently now. I know I was made for work. One of the exercises you'll do later is to write down all the people God has asked you to care for in your home. You can know, without a doubt, that God has given you the work of caring for those people and taking care of your home. Give thanks to God that He has chosen you for this work. Then set about to try and change your attitude about the work you must do.

Embrace Suffering

"Everything that has being comes from God. Nothing, therefore, that happens to us — trouble or temptation or injury or torment or slander or anything else that could possibly happen to us — can or will disturb us. Rather, we are content and hold these things in reverence, reflecting that they come from God and are given to us as good favors, not out of hatred but out of love."
— St. Catherine of Siena

I did not grow up Catholic and I was not taught how to suffer. There actually is a proper way to suffer, and that is to combine our suffering with the suffering that Jesus went through on the Cross. This is called redemptive suffering.

This concept is one of my favorite parts of being Catholic and one of the biggest theological ideas that the Protestants miss out on. We believe, as Catholics, that when we suffer and offer up that suffering, it has real power and real meaning.

In Jeff Cavins' book *When You Suffer*, he says:

> "I'll show you how all of us have an opportunity for our daily lives to be transformed, whether it is through intense suffering or a dull, nagging type of suffering. When life gets uncomfortable, unpredictable, when you feel weak and empty — that's exactly when you have an opportunity to become more like Christ.
>
> Nothing [is] lacking in Christ's sufferings, but so that we might know the love of God more deeply, Christ has made room in his suffering for us to participate in it.
>
> That means that when you are in union with Christ and you offer up your suffering in union with Him, your suffering is redeemed. You are valuable — so valuable that Christ wanted to redeem even your suffering and make it meaningful in your life. Our suffering united to Christ trumps any less-than-ideal day."[12]

This is a difficult concept to wrestle with sometimes. When you break your arm, you may say the words, "I offer this pain up to Jesus." If you say this, however, and then spend the rest of the day being grouchy to everyone, you have missed the point. We should offer up our suffering to Jesus and then endure it quietly.

This doesn't mean we shouldn't ask for help or ask people to pray for us. It means we should be polite and pleasant when we're going through a trial. I blow this all the time. Sometimes I can't wait for my husband to come home so I can tell him all the awful things I've had to do that day. While a husband should support his wife, that's no excuse for me to turn him into an emotional dumpster every day when he comes home from work.

We should take a cue from Mary who suffered Jesus's crucifixion by silently weeping. Mary was good at suffering; she is always our perfect model. She teaches us that we must endure the suffering of others, too. Sometimes watching someone we love suffer is harder than our own suffering. It is wrong of us, however, to watch the suffering of others and feel that it is senseless, worthless, or unfair. God is doing a great work in them, and we must trust Him.

Knowing that suffering has value doesn't mean that we shouldn't pray and ask that it be removed. Even Jesus asked His great Father if this cup could pass from Him. But after we have sent up our prayers, it is important that we embrace our suffering and know that it is God's way of showing us how much He loves us. He allowed his Son to go through the worst possible suffering so that our sins would be forgiven. He allows our own suffering as a chance to participate in that redemption.

Marguerite Duportals who wrote *How To Make Sense of Suffering*, said:

> "In the sacred commerce that God permits a soul to carry on with Him, pain acquires value of the highest order, in fact becomes the noblest of values. Suffering becomes a power. Those who suffer, those who are afflicted are the really wealthy people of this world. They are rich, but frequently they do not know how to spend it."[13]

Understanding redemptive suffering helped me make significant progress in my own life, especially around my negative attitude. I could write a whole book about redemptive suffering, but the good news is, lots of people already have, including my fabulous editor Jeannie Ewing, author of *From Grief to Grace*[14]! There are many good books you can read about this topic if you need to grow in this area.

There is nothing in my life that has taught me the value of suffering more than miscarriage. I have experienced three miscarriages in the last five years. The last one was after 12 weeks, which was extremely painful and emotionally heartbreaking. I imagine every woman who has gone through this has lifted her face to the sky and, through streaming tears, asked, "Why God? Why has this happened?"

Losing a child can feel like such a tragic event. It's hard to see the good in such a dark situation. Lord help the women who experience this without faith in Jesus. I'm not sure I could have held on to myself or my marriage without leaning on the Lord. It was in these dark times, however, that I learned to trust God. I had to believe in His plan and I had to lean on the idea of redemptive suffering to make it through - to make sense of what I had to endure.

One last thing I want to say about redemptive suffering, is that while Catholics believe you can offer up your suffering for a specific intention (e.g. your marriage, unborn babies, the salvation of a loved one etc.), when you consecrate yourself to Mary through Jesus, you no longer choose what to offer up your suffering for. Instead, you give all your good works and your suffering to Mary. She decides how best to distribute them.

I thought it would bother me not to be able to state an intention for my offerings, but instead, I have found great joy in the idea. Now when I have a splitting headache, I offer it up to Mary, and I know she will redeem that suffering for the most appropriate person or cause in that very moment. I am pleased to know my suffering is being used in the best way instead of my own self-centered ways. Sometimes I still choose a personal intention to focus on. I know my intention may not be what Mary "spends" my suffering on but it still gives me strength to endure the suffering.

Do not fear your suffering.

Throughout this book, I'm going to ask you to embrace hard work and to lean into your suffering. I promise, though, if you can make a paradigm shift in your own life so you no longer fear work and suffering, you will make huge strides in becoming the person God wants you to be. You will find a greater peace than you have ever known.

Obviously, there are many topics related to our Catholic faith that I have not covered. This section was never meant to be a comprehensive theology lesson. Rather, my hope was to point you to five practices that will deepen your faith life. If you can make God your best friend, go through Marian consecration, have a strong prayer life, embrace work, and endure suffering, you will have a great deal more peace when dealing with the other six facets of your life.

Chapter Two:
Marriage

"Teach us to give and not count the cost."
– St. Ignatius de Loyola

Just as we are called to become saints in Heaven, the purpose of marriage is to help get our spouse to Heaven, too. When trying to balance raising little kids, making sure dinner is on the table, sticking to our budget, and surviving *life*, it's hard to see what getting my husband to Heaven even looks like!

My husband and I come from broken and divorced families. Because of our rocky start in life, we both knew that we didn't know anything about marriage. We didn't pretend for one minute that we knew what a healthy marriage looked like. It was easy for us to set down our pride and ask for help. We started by reading Catholic books about marriage.

A common theme you will notice, when I talk about each of the seven facets of life, is that I want you to acknowledge the things that you don't know. Being prideful is one of the biggest sins that keeps us from growing. When we won't admit to ourselves that things aren't working, or won't be humble enough to seek out information, it's easy to get stuck in toxic behaviors.

We allow limiting beliefs to hold us back. Here are some common lies that we tell ourselves:

"Nothing can possibly help me. My situation is hopeless."

"Well I've always been this way, I'm never going to change."

"You haven't met my husband; he would never agree to try that."

"Only people with money can do that."

"I'm too stupid to understand that."

"I have no time to learn something new."

"My marriage is fine just the way it is."

I tell myself limiting beliefs all the time. And when I'm really frustrated, sometimes I say them out loud to my husband. These are usually times when I'm stressed, hungry, tired, or at the end of my rope. Even though they sound reasonable in the moment, they are still just lies.

I've gotten better at noticing limiting beliefs and not letting them take root in my heart. My husband and I have also learned how to more gently point out each other's limiting beliefs. We have learned to tread lightly here because limiting beliefs tend to pop up in times of tension. It is our job as married people to help each other achieve sanctification so we can't give up.

Sometimes that means being a shoulder to cry on and supporting your spouse without words, perhaps with a simple hug. Sometimes that means saying something challenging to help your spouse grow. The more my husband and I affirm each other and our mission to get each other into heaven, the easier it has become for us to help each other grow toward becoming the best-version-of-ourselves. That's an awfully hard thing to do in the first year of marriage. We have gotten so much better at this over the years, so please, if you're a newlywed, don't be too hard on yourself. It gets better!

I couldn't possibly delve into the complexities, struggles and huge blessings of marriage in a few pages. Instead, I'm going to focus on three practices all couples should be doing to maintain a strong marriage: get right with God, focus on growth and maintain a physical connection.

Get Right With God

*"Understanding is the reward of faith. Therefore seek not
to understand that you may believe, but believe that you
may understand."*
–St. Augustine

I remember the first time I thought, "I don't think I can be married to him forever!" It's a startling and deeply disturbing thought to have after you've already gotten married. My husband and I are both devout Christians, so the idea of divorce was simply not on the table. I don't even remember what had happened that day, but suddenly I felt paralyzed by the idea that this man, *who clearly didn't love me or understand me at all*, was going to be my partner for the rest of my life!

No one tells you that you might have ugly thoughts about your spouse. I never imagined the blissful intimacy we shared could someday feel shattered. I wish someone would have explained that while the devil tries to do everything to get you to have sex before you are married, he spends the same amount of energy keeping you *from* having sex after you're married. I wasn't prepared for the level of stress six pregnancies in five years would put on us. Gone were our carefree days of walks in the park. The laughter had died and I wasn't sure it would ever come back.

Marriage is hard work. It can feel like a battlefield. Throw in a few kids who take away some of your freedom and you're left sitting in your living room, staring at your husband, wondering how marriage quickly turned into a place that feels like a prison.

These are harsh words, I know. Over time we found tools to help us, some of which I will mention later. We have had many moments of joy and laughter since that first big argument. I can't even remember what it was about and we would go on to have many more, what I call "adjustments." As we melded our lives together, we needed to adjust our attitudes, our expectations, and even our wants.

I have come to view marriage as one of the most beautiful and fulfilling journeys someone can take. Marriage is filled with countless blessings and the most amazing graces. I find great satisfaction when my husband and I are aligned. He will be my partner for as long as we both shall live, even as we hit some landmines along the way.

I'd be lying if I only shared the happy moments I've had with my husband. It would be a disservice to you to pretend that even healthy marriages don't go through hard times.

The Catholic Mom Challenge is about facing reality and growing in each area of our life. Growing in our marriage is the second most important thing we will do with our entire lives! We cannot be naive about the challenges we will face in our marriages. We must acknowledge them and seek out resources to help us grow.

A broken marriage cannot live in the background. It will poison all the other areas of your life. If your marriage is broken, if you and your husband are fighting all the time or stonewalling each other, it's going to be very hard to make progress in the other facets of your life.

If you are unhappy in your marriage, or you feel like something isn't working, the first thing you need to do is to evaluate where you are spiritually. Are you partaking in the sacraments? Are you praying every single day? Even if your husband is not Catholic, you should be making these practices a priority.

It's very difficult for God to heal your marriage if you're not doing these basic Catholic activities. Of course, God can help you in any situation. This is not a quid pro quo kind of relationship. Rather, God already has a plan for you. He may even be trying to speak some truth into your heart, but if your heart is closed and your hands are over your ears, you're not going to hear His plan.

If you have let your Catholic faith fade, immediately set out to strengthen your relationship with God. Lay your marriage troubles at the foot of the Cross. Cry out to Him for help. Then, spend some time in silence and really listen to what the Lord has to say.

Here are some ways you can reconnect with our Lord:

- Read your Bible (Start with the gospels or the Proverbs every single day)
- Pray your rosary
- Go to Adoration
- Attend daily Mass one day per week, if possible
- Choose a patron saint for your marriage and ask for his/her intercession
- Pray a novena (*Our Lady Undoer of Knots* is my favorite for marriage)
- Go to Confession

Get right with God, then ask yourself, "What am I doing to help my marriage grow?"

Focus on Growth

Coming from divorced parents, I didn't have a clue how to be married. I bought books and read them early on to try and find a model I could aim for. In Gregory Popcak's *For Better...Forever*[15], he asks couples to make a list of 25 things you can do to make your spouse feel loved and appreciated. It was fun to make this list. I was in a happy place and I cheerily thought of the little special things that I could do for my husband.

I never imagined that later, I would want to crumple that list. *Why should I have to do something nice for him first? He's been so awful lately, I couldn't possibly make his favorite dinner.*

I hope that sounds childish to you because it is. I completely understand that, in the moment, when our feelings are bruised, it can be hard to want to be nice to our spouse. Actually, it can feel downright impossible. Remember, though, love begins when the feelings are gone. One of the best ways to repair your marriage is to serve your spouse.

When your marriage feels like it's covered in slime, it's a lot easier to see all the ways you wish your husband would change. It's very difficult to force your spouse to grow, however. One of the most effective ways to change your marriage is to serve your spouse more. I know this can be extremely difficult if you're hurt and feeling unloved. This is still where you need to start.

Just about every marriage book I've ever read says something similar. If you haven't read a Catholic book about marriage, I highly recommend starting there. Check one out at the library or download an audio book (many of which are free on YouTube.)

You can read articles from *Focus On The Family* or listen to More2Life on the radio or at Ave Maria Radio. There are plenty of resources out there.

Keep reading and learning until you can make a list of things you can do to show your spouse that you love him. I keep a list handy in my office. Yes, that list I made when I was in a good mood. This helps me so I don't have to try and come up with the ideas when I was in a grumpy mood.

Here are some of my favorite ways to love my husband and to serve him better as a wife:

- Remember that he wants respect. I'll thumb through *Love and Respect*[16] again for ideas on how to show him the respect he wants.
- Speak his love language, which is physical touch. This doesn't always mean sex. He likes long hugs, holding hands, and a quick kiss when I come into the room. I don't naturally think to do these things, but I work on them because it really speaks to him.
- I'll make a list of a few things that I know bug him around the house, and I'll take care of them. It's easy to only fix the things that bug me, but out of love and service, I know how to step things up in a way that makes him happy.
- Smile more. A lot of times he'll say, "All I want is a happy wife." I'm a sarcastic, grumpy melancholic by nature, so it takes extra effort to smile and be cheery. I'll give myself a little pep talk before he comes home. It's not fake. I genuinely love him, and he works so hard for our family. I can give him a smile and a happy attitude when he comes home.
- Tell him what I need. Men can be dense. They are not women, and they are not mind readers. Sometimes all he needs is for me to *tell him what I want*, and then he's happy to do it.
- Pray for him. When I don't know what to do, I just pray for him. I do this anyway, but if we're in a rough patch or I'm feeling frustrated, I set aside additional time to just pray for him and our marriage.
- Read a book about marriage. I just ask a good group of Catholic ladies on Facebook what they like, and I pick one I haven't read.
- Plan a date night. Even if it's spaghetti at home, I just plan something, light some candles, and create a space to connect.

If you're thinking to yourself, *I have no idea how to love my husband and what speaks to him*, that's okay. Your first job is to figure that out. It's helpful to take some personality tests, either together, or separately, so you can understand each other's personalities and natural tendencies better. Here are some I recommend:

- The Five Love Languages[17]
- The Temperament God Gave Your Spouse[18]
- Meyers-Briggs Personality Test[19]
- Talk to think vs Think to talk[20]

The important thing is that we don't settle for "good enough." We don't accept that it's "always going to be this way." Though we should embrace suffering, "just offer it up" isn't a solution to marriage challenges. Sure, we can do that along the way, but we need to be proactive in working on our marriages and strengthening them.

If things are really rocky, go see a priest either by yourself or together as a couple, if your husband is willing. Later in the book, I'll talk more about ways to make progress when you've got a grumpy spouse who won't budge.

If you think things are going smoothly, that's wonderful. That doesn't mean there aren't aspects you can improve. Neither of you are saints yet, so there's probably something you can work on. Make sure you do not get so consumed with your job, your children, or even your church activities that your marriage fades into the background.

God called you to the vocation of marriage. Take it seriously. Make time to work on your marriage. It will be very hard to make progress in the other facets of your life if your marriage is either on fire or completely frozen.

Maintain a Physical Connection

The devil tries his hardest to get us to have pre-marital sex and then turns around trying to keep us from having sex once we're married. Sexual intimacy is a vital part of marriage and so often we get this beautiful part of our relationship wrong. Our world has been so invaded by toxic messages about our bodies and what sex should look like, that many of us end up confused in our own marriage beds!

To be honest, I don't have a lot of advice to offer here. I'm still struggling to figure out my sex life with my husband. We got pregnant on our honeymoon so our *magical* first year of marriage was filled with morning sickness, exhaustion, uncomfortable sleeping and then finally a newborn. Second-trimester second honeymoon? That didn't happen for me.

I have been pregnant or postpartum for most of our five years of marriage. I have struggled with vaginismus, which means sex is often painful for me. What should be a love-filled, marriage-affirming activity for us, is often filled with anxiety and confusion.

I say this because even though I kind of feel like I have an awful sex life, I still believe that sex is a crucial part of marriage. I know that even though my husband and I have struggled to figure out how to be intimate and to receive these graces that all the books promise, we keep trying.

We know the answer could never be to just stop having sex. God does call some couples to long-term abstinence for special reasons, but I don't feel like that is the case in my marriage. Instead, we just have a lot of work to do. We both have brokenness from previous sexual relationships before our conversions. I don't know if we're still repairing that brokenness. Sometimes I wonder if we're going through this so we can share our story later and help other couples who have similar challenges.

It doesn't matter. What matters is that we continue to be physical with each other. We have to keep hugging, kissing, spooning and yes, trying to have sex. It's very difficult to nurture a marriage without touch.

My husband's love language is physical touch, which happens to be my lowest scoring love language. The idea that he wants to hold hands or cuddle on the couch, is outside of my comfort zone. It doesn't come naturally to me. I have to remind myself to give him a kiss when he walks into the kitchen. I don't kiss him begrudgingly, I kiss him because I love him deeply. It just takes work for me to remember this.

Conversely, my husband could care less about receiving gifts. He has to go out of his way to think, "Pick up a gift for Sterling at the store because that makes her happy." It's hard for him to believe that I feel loved by receiving gifts because this has such little meaning for him.

Even if you've taken the Love Languages test[21] and neither of you scores high on physical touch, it's still an important part of marriage. Humans were made to be touched. Perhaps you have a crazy schedule. Perhaps your children are always around. Perhaps the only time you two have a moment of peace is at the end of the day when you're too tired to think.

The reasons don't matter. If you go long periods of time without touching each other, your relationship will suffer.

It's not sexy to have to schedule time to kiss your husband or to be intimate but if that's what you have to do in this season of life, then do it. Letting your marriage wither because you are busy is a mistake.

Take heart, God can do amazing things. No matter how broken your marriage is, no matter how hopeless you feel, he can do miracles. He really can and He does.

Don't stop fighting for your marriage. Don't stop praying for your marriage. Don't let your marriage get stale and stay that way. Turn to the Holy Family. Pray to Jesus, Mary and Joseph for help. Pray to all the saints! You have a wealth of Catholic treasure available to you. Partake in the sacraments and lean on those who are in Heaven.

Marriage is a holy thing and yours can be healed.

Chapter Three: Motherhood

*"It is not hard to obey when we love the one
whom we obey."*
– St. Ignatius of Loyola

This quote inspires me, but it is not about children. Instead, it inspires me to obey God, out of my deep love for Him. He has asked me to raise Catholic children, and I will do my very best because of my love for him.

It's a frightening endeavor to write about motherhood because of the mommy wars, the millions of blog articles, and the endless permutations of how we can raise our children. Out of fear, many of us strive to keep the peace by saying, "I'm okay, you're okay, we're all okay." I think the biggest danger here is in co-signing bad behavior.

I'm not going to specifically name what I think bad behavior is because inevitably there will be someone whose life situation is such that my advice wouldn't apply. Instead, I want to challenge you to examine your own vocation of motherhood. Later on in the book, I'm going to ask you to write a Mission Statement for this facet of your life. You're going to describe what being a perfect mother would look like for you.

Even the phrase "perfect mother" feels charged. We are called to sainthood. There is a perfect combination of all of the gifts that God has given us and how we use those gifts to raise our children. While we will never achieve perfect motherhood, we should always be aiming for it.

I personally think of it as trying to win my own MOTHER OF THE YEAR AWARD, and I'm competing with all the different versions of myself. There are three things that are crucial for us to practice as we live out our vocation of motherhood: do your best (checking in often), commit to virtues training, and schedule time for daily personal prayer.

Do Your Best (Checking In Often)

Most of us know when we're not doing our best. I could ask you right now for five simple ways you could to improve how you are parenting, and you would quickly come up with five answers. The problem is not that we don't *know* how to be good parents, it's that we struggle to actually *do* the good things we know we ought to do.

You know when you are not doing your best. You don't need to beat yourself up about it; you don't need to dwell on it; you don't need to throw yourself a pity party or wallow in sadness. Acknowledge that it wasn't your best, make a plan to do better, and move on. Don't accept your own apathy.

When I'm in my first-trimester pregnancy and I'm throwing up all the time, "best" looks a lot different than when my youngest is two and I'm in a good place spiritually, financially, and physically. I'm not asking you to be a super human; I'm asking you to assess your current situation and to ask yourself, "Am I doing my best?"

Michael Hyatt has a great analogy about life planning[22]. He says you should create a life plan, which is like plugging an address into your GPS. If during your day, you get off the most efficient path, your GPS will respond by saying, "recalculating route."

I'm asking you to envision yourself at your best and plug that vision into your life GPS. The Catholic Mom Challenge system will have you check in with yourself often and assess if you have gotten off the best path. If you have, you will recalculate your route to get back on track.

You're going to blow it all the time.

I blow it all the time. As I'm writing this very paragraph, I haven't showered in three days. I got sucked into work for an hour-and-a-half this morning when I was supposed to be reading books to my kids. I'm in the middle of trying to lose weight, but I had three pieces of garlic bread at a party last night. I say this because those things used to crater me. They would make me feel like a failure, and I would spiral down into depression and self-loathing.

Now, I quickly turn to my Catholic Mom Manifesto for consolation and ideas to get out of my funk. First, I find prayers to Mary and Jesus, as well as quotes from the saints. I soak up God's love and His wisdom. Then I look at the tips section of my booklet for ideas and here's what I did to get back on track:

- I played *Sorry* with my kids, which is a sacrifice, because I can't stand it (though they love it;)
- I texted my husband and told him that I need him to watch the kids later so I could take a shower;
- Later that evening, I made a meal plan for the week to get me back on track.

Boom.

I turned things around quickly. I recalculated my route and moved forward. This is what I'm asking you to do with your vocation of motherhood. Of course, it's going to change all the time. Of course, it's not going to go smoothly every day. I'm asking you to be committed to checking in with yourself often and making a plan to get back to that best-version-of-yourself.

Virtues Training

"Temperance is a disposition that restrains our desires for things which it is base to desire."
–St. Augustine

I was completely unprepared to be a mother. Having no Catholic background, only one sibling, and having grown up with a single mom in a tiny apartment, I had received most of my life lessons from the school of hard knocks. I knew of virtues in a Disney-ified Jiminy Cricket sort of way. Later, I would be introduced to virtues in a Benjamin Franklin kind of way. But I had very little knowledge of how to live out the virtues myself or how to train up my children to live virtuous lives.

Lord help the young moms who pick up *The Story of a Soul* and think, "My children aren't anything like the St. Therese, Little Flower, I'm doomed!" But even sweet Therese, who wanted so badly to give her whole life to the Lord at a very young age, struggled in virtue when she was a young child. It was the constant training and practice of virtues that her parents provided that helped her set down her selfish tendencies and turn toward God.

Few of us will have children quite like Therese, but we have an opportunity to train the children we do have to live a life of virtue. Virtues include working hard, being kind, exercising self-control and being humble. These are the traits we want all our children to have by the time we send them out into the world.

Moms struggle to teach virtue because many of us were never taught how to live virtuous lives. We need to study virtues so we can pass that knowledge on to our children. And though we are striving for sainthood, being a saint isn't contingent upon being perfectly virtuous. Most of the saints were terrible sinners who struggled with virtue. As we seek to become more like Jesus, it makes sense that we use virtues as guideposts.

When we are charitable, we become more like Christ.

When we practice prudence, we become more like Christ.

When we are kind and loving, we become more like Christ.

When we are chaste and honest, we become more like Christ.

I am currently designing a virtues training program for both children and adults so we can work on these skills together as a family. I firmly believe that if we focused more on virtues training instead of winning gold stars and trophies, we would bear the fruits of the spirit. We would be Jesus's hands in the world.

One virtue mothers need to teach their children is obedience. Too often, children are compliant merely to avoid a punishment. While I think discipline and punishments are good tools for parents, if the children are never taught the real meaning behind obedience, they will struggle to obey the Lord in their adulthood.

We must train them up in virtue. It will take a lot of practice. There will be tears. There will be rebellion, but we cannot let the children rule us with their emotions. It's easy to let kids walk all over us. I know I'm guilty of this often, especially when I'm tired. But it is a disservice to our children when we don't discipline them or develop their virtues.

It's important that we remember that virtue is always the center point between two vices. There is a danger in either extreme.

When we love too much, it becomes enablement.

When we are too diligent, we become workaholics.

When we practice temperance to excess, it becomes strictness.

Mothers need to become familiar with virtues themselves in order to be able to teach them. My family currently uses the *We Choose Virtues* program[23], which is based on Christian (though not specifically Catholic) teaching. My kids really enjoy it and it pleases me to see their patience, kindness, and use of words like "perseverance."

Teaching virtues, however, is not enough. We must also discipline our children when they are making bad choices. Some bad choices have natural consequences, like when my daughter won't sit in the middle of her chair so she falls off the edge onto the floor. Some bad choices, like lying, require discipline from the parents to help children learn they are unacceptable. While it may seem that lying has few consequences in the real world, we, as parents, must educate them about the spiritual consequences of such behaviors. We can help them understand the short-sightedness of taking the easy, but wrong, way out.

Discipline teaches children self-control. I know I struggle with self-control. Why would I want my children to struggle with this in their adulthood, too? If I can give them the gift of learning how to control their impulses, it will ease their way in the world. They will be freer to focus on Christ and carry out His will.

It would be impossible for me to lay out a discipline plan that would cover all the different temperaments, motivations and mental capacities of children. Instead, I will simply say that discipline must be part of your family. Find a way to parent and train your children. This is a great task that God has assigned to you. Don't let your children take advantage of you because it's uncomfortable to parent them. Consider their adulthood. If they still suffer from the same lack of discipline, it will hurt them far more in the future than if you ground them or give them extra chores now.

It is hard to train children in virtue and to discipline them but God gives us the grace to do this. One way that we can access more and more of this grace, is to have a strong prayer life.

It Comes Down To Prayer

"Devotion is a certain act of the will by which man gives himself promptly to divine service."
—St. Thomas Aquinas

I remember the first time I read Holly Pierlot's *Mother's Rule of Life*[24]. Her structured day, peppered with Hail Marys and Divine Mercy, seemed overwhelming and impossible for me to accomplish! It sounded too rigid and a little too unrealistic. At the time, I only had one child, so I hadn't yet realized that the more children you have, and the busier you are, the easier it is to implement systems.

The fuller my life becomes, the easier it has been to put boxes around our many activities and to-do lists. I actually find more joy and satisfaction out of the structure now that we have three children. I'm also more motivated to enforce this structure because the resulting chaos of not planning would be much more painful.

After having three children, I found my life looking a lot more like *A Mother's Rule of Life*[25]. We do laundry every Monday and Thursday. We have morning time with books and songs. We pick up the playroom before nap and before bedtime. This structured schedule we keep wouldn't be possible without consistent prayer.

Much like Holly says, my school and chore routines wouldn't be possible if it wasn't for my strong prayer life. I make time in the morning and all throughout the day, and again at night, to pray. This time is set aside for Jesus. It is a time of talking and listening to Him.

If you are too busy to pray, then you are too busy. Cut some things out immediately or learn to pair prayer with activities you can't get rid of (e.g. taking a shower, folding laundry, etc.)

Make it a priority to pray every single day. I pray all throughout the day because that helps me keep my heart in tune with Christ. It gives me the grace and strength to get through the rest of the day. Many of the motherhood quotes you'll read in Appendix B have to do with prayer and leaning on God. Here is one example from St. Charles Borromeo:

> "We must meditate before, during and after everything we do. The prophet says: 'I will pray, and then I will understand.' This is the way we can easily overcome the countless difficulties we have to face day after day, which, after all, are part of our work. In meditation we find the strength to bring Christ to birth in ourselves and in others." - Saint Charles Borromeo[26]

A large part of motherhood seems to be fighting the urge to worry and be anxious. We have been put in charge of raising these beautiful little souls, and we just want to get it right. We want our children to be healthy, happy, and faithful and we're so worried we're going to mess it up. But God asks us over and over again to not be afraid. He gives us peace and promises us that He will keep giving us peace.

He does not say, "Try not to be so anxious, Sterling."

He says, "Be anxious for nothing." *Nothing.*

I'm still pretty far from that.

Be anxious for nothing.

I'm convinced the only way we can do this is by praying all the time. There are plenty of books and websites about the many different ways that you can pray. Don't get caught up in the wrong or right way to do it and let that keep you from actually praying.

Just talk to Jesus like he is your Friend, your Abba Father, the One who created you. He loves you so much and wants to hear everything you have to say. Pray often and remind yourself to stop worrying. This is an important part of living out our vocation of motherhood with contentment. I often contemplate this quote from Elizabeth Ann Seton when I'm trying to connect my vocation of motherhood to the Lord.

> *"The first end I propose in our daily work is to do the will of God; secondly, to do it in the manner He wills it; and thirdly to do it because it is His will."*
> *Saint Elizabeth Ann Seton*

For Those of You With Lost Kids

*"I know well that the greater and more beautiful the work
is, the more terrible will be the storms
that rage against it."*
– St. Faustina

Some of you have grown children who have fallen away from the church or are living with their boyfriends or addicted to drugs. Some of you may have children living in your house who have already forsaken all of your good teachings and won't listen to you anymore. Perhaps some of you are converts, and you didn't raise your children with the faith or values you have now, and you're feeling bad about the choices they're making.

You feel as if you've already taken and failed the motherhood test, and it's over. But that's not true at all. I know this because I was once a lost child as well.

First of all, the salvation of your children is not ultimately on you. God does not ask you to save your children. Every child has to make that choice on their own as adults. It does not help or change anything for you to sit and feel guilty about what you have done in the past. Maybe you did totally screw it up, but their salvation is not on you. Go to Confession.

God does not desire us to carry guilt or anxiety. Leave it at the foot of the cross.

The best thing to do right now is to become a prayer warrior. A prayer warrior is someone who prays often and very deeply with their heart. I've had the great pleasure of seeing Sr. Miriam James Heidland of the Society of Our Lady of the Most Holy Trinity speak two times. Her testimony is extremely powerful. She was a fallen away Catholic. She became an alcoholic in college and was enjoying the raucous life of a collegiate athlete. Her mother, at her wit's end and brokenhearted, didn't know what to do.

One night, Sr. Miriam's mother went into the basement of their home and kneeled on the floor in front of a statue of our Blessed Mother. Crying, she told the Blessed Mother that her daughter was lost and there was nothing she could do. She asked our Blessed Mother to pray for her daughter's conversion. In a story of amazing grace, it wasn't long before her daughter became Sr. Miriam. It's an incredible story, which you can read in *Loved As I Am* by Sr. Miriam,[27] a book I highly recommend.

Prayer is powerful. I was very far from the church in my early twenties when my mom converted to Christianity. I didn't know it at the time, but my mom's new prayer group prayed for me regularly. I swore I would never be religious as I thought Jesus was a crux for weak people. God had a different plan, however, because the prayers of that faithful group were answered. I became a passionate Christian at the age of twenty-two.

I would go on to become Catholic at the age of twenty-five. There is yet time. Be patient and trust in the Lord.

Sometimes the only thing we can do is pray. If you are crying about how many mistakes you have made but have not yet gotten on your knees and prayed to our Blessed Mother, you are not doing all that you can. Ask for her intercession.

God asks us to have faith. He tells us that Mary is our mother. She is the best person to ask for help. She will listen to your heart, and as a mother, she will know the deep pain that you are feeling. Ask for her intercession. Pray the Rosary every day. If you are going to cry, cry out to her and beg for her son's mercy. Faith can do amazing things.

Have faith. Lay your worries at the foot of the Cross and then just have faith. Sometimes the only thing you can do as a mother is pray. Make sure you're at least doing that.

Spiritual Motherhood

"Listen and attend with the ear of your heart."
– St. Benedict

This book is clearly targeted to Catholic mothers, but I also wanted it to be something that a woman who didn't have children could also benefit from. It's important to know that even if God hasn't called you to have physical children or to foster or adopt children in your home, that God has called you to be a spiritual mother.

Spiritual motherhood is sometimes a confusing concept. Even when we hear that phrase thrown around, many of us don't know what it actually means. God created women to nurture. That doesn't mean we are all warm, cookie baking, arms open wide women. I actually don't do that kind of nurturing very easily. I'm not naturally good with children, kissing boo-boos, or feeling comfortable watching someone cry in front of me.

Nurturing is about helping something to grow. It comes naturally to me to help people grow in business and to achieve their dreams. Some of us are called to help others to grow in their emotional, spiritual, moral, or cultural lives.

You have a special gift from God that helps you nurture others in a certain way. Whether you have biological children or not, you need to find the people in your life that God is asking you to nurture. Here are some ways you may be called to spiritual motherhood:

- Getting involved at church;
- Being a mentor for students;
- Supporting a civil rights movement;
- Campaigning for a moral-political issue;
- Helping pregnant teens find resources;
- Creating harmony with your extended family;
- Organizing your neighbors to serve each other more;
- Volunteering for underprivileged children;
- Offering art classes to senior citizens.

If you are not sure how God is calling you to be a spiritual mother, then start praying about it. Say this prayer every day:

"God, send me spiritual children and help my heart to be open to serve them."

God created women to be incredibly beautiful, powerful, and nurturing. Discover the gifts that He has given you and share them with the world. This will be deeply satisfying and fulfilling even if it is outside of your comfort zone.

Chapter Four:
Rest

*"When you encounter difficulties and contradictions, do
not try to break them, but bend them with
gentleness and time."*
—St. Francis de Sales

Since all the facets of our life are founded on our faith, it is always a priority for us. None of the six facets are firmly more important than the others. Circumstances may come up that make any one of the six facets your main focus.

For example, if your house has gotten so messy that you can't open your front door and it has actually become a hazard to live there, then homemaking should likely be your top priority. I know a Mom who suffered from postpartum depression and actually got to this place. In her situation, it wasn't the right moment to say, "Marriage is really important; you should schedule a weekly date night."

No, she needed some serious help from her friends to get her house cleaned so it wasn't a danger to her children. Then she needed to get some counseling and maybe even some medication to help her back on track.

While I think marriage is the most common facet to be left in the background, rest is the next most common facet that suffers, for women especially.

Ladies, most of us are terrible at resting! I don't mean falling into bed and sleeping because you're exhausted at the end of the day. I mean the actual kind of self-care that rejuvenates your body and spirit.

God very clearly wants us to work, but He also wants us to rest. "Make holy the Sabbath." It's an actual commandment; the fourth one. And to be honest, many of us don't even know how to do that. We're so caught up in getting things done that the only kind of rest we know is drinking a glass of wine and going to bed long after our bedtime. Maybe we'll sneak an episode of our favorite show before.

This isn't the kind of rest that sustains us.

We need a plan to create actual rest in our lives. What are the activities that give you renewed energy? For some of you, taking a walk is very restful. I have a friend who absolutely loves running five miles. While running five miles would cause me anxiety and dread, it actually brings her peace and rest. When she is done, she feels alive and rejuvenated.

The activities that restore us will be different for each one of us. The important thing is to pay attention to what actually fills up your energy tank and makes you feel ready to tackle your life. Later, I'll ask you to make a list of five things you think are restful. You'll try them out a few times and then check in with yourself. Did they really make you feel better, or did you feel worse somehow?

This might seem like a silly activity, but many of us are confused about which activities actually bring us rest. Also, these activities may change over time.

Find Effective Ways to Rest

*"Our body has this defect that, the more it is provided
care and comforts, the more needs and desires it finds."*
—St. Teresa of Avila

I'm the queen of picking bad things to do in my downtime. I know that watching Netflix, checking social media, or playing games on my phone leaves me overstimulated. I think these activities are restful because they make me feel good. All those things feel good, however, because they release dopamine in my system. I'm getting a little fix every time I do one of these activities.[28]

Our body craves these little pings so we think about them; we become excited. We know they're going to feel good. But these activities aren't actually rejuvenating. In many cases, they're actually draining.

Ineffective ways to relax that often don't work:

- Social media;
- Checking email;
- Watching television;
- Reading or watching the news;
- Playing games on your phone;
- Just about most things that involve blue screens or notifications.

None of these activities actually help your brain recover in the end. They aren't actually relaxing. None of these activities help you recharge. That's why you can spend your kids' nap time on Facebook and still not feel rested at all. Your eyes will feel a little sore; you're grumpier and you don't feel ready to tackle the difficult, late afternoon hours with your children.

Effective ways to relax include:

- Reading;
- Spending time outside;
- Light exercise;
- Stretching;
- Planned prayer;
- Breathing deeply;
- Knitting, gardening, cooking, or some other hobby you enjoy.

Some people find knitting or gardening relaxing. Gardening really stresses me out. I hate bugs, and my fair skin makes it uncomfortable to be in the sun. Some people enjoy coloring or cooking. I actually find folding laundry quiet and soothing. I discovered this in my adulthood. My kids see me folding laundry, and they run the other way, so it's a time of real peace and quiet for me.

Just think of whatever puts you in that quiet place – image ocean waves lapping in the background. Do those things and not the fake things listed above. It will make a huge difference in your ability to recharge and you will have more energy for longer in the day.

Schedule Your Rest

"If we wish to make any progress in the service of God we must begin every day of our life with new eagerness."
– St. Charles Borromeo

It's difficult to experience deep rest without planning, so it's important to put rest time on your calendar. Coordinate with your spouse, let your kids know what's going on and carve out time where you are not to be disturbed.

You may be in a busy season of life where you can only manage five to fifteen minutes of rest. Don't be discouraged by this. Don't let bitterness keep you from enjoying even a small window of rest. Sometimes, because I feel sorry for myself, I ruin my own chances of enjoying the time I do manage to get. It's self-destructive to continually proclaim you're too busy to rest and then miss out on the five-minute opportunities when you can.

Last month, when my hair was on fire and I felt I was drowning, I would try to take five minutes and sit on the swinging bench we have in our backyard. Sometimes, I would only get three minutes before my business phone would ring or the kids would need something. I would try, however, to give myself over to those short, three minutes. I would breathe deeply, be present, and really commit to resting in those moments.

Put it on your calendar. If your husband doesn't understand why you need a little you time, tell him that you need rest in order to improve all the other facets of your life. Your husband wants you to be a happy wife. He wants you to be a good mother to your kids. He wants your home to run smoothly. Tell him that the key to doing these things is to recharge your batteries.

Seasons of Rest

Sometimes there are seasons when you need to take it easy. Recuperating after pregnancy, or surgery, are the first two that come to my mind. In an effort to maintain control and to see that things are done perfectly, moms often short-change themselves on the rest they need. I remember leaving the hospital with my firstborn and being proud as I waddled through Babies "R" Us to pick out some last minute things we needed.

"Look how strong I am?" I thought.

Recovery from that pregnancy was the hardest of my three full-term pregnancies. It took a long time. Looking back, I think it took longer than necessary because I was too stubborn to stay in bed in those first days. I was prideful about my ability to be productive; I did not value being a healthy mama for my new baby girl.

By the time my third daughter came, I had told all my friends and family that it was my intention to stay in my room for a whole week. I wanted to rest and cuddle my new baby so we could focus on resting, bonding, and breastfeeding. I didn't feel bad about this for a second and I didn't spend a minute worrying about food, laundry or the other children. I knew everything would be fine, even if it wasn't how I would manage things. Since my husband had just started a new job, he actually only had a week off of work, which was much less than we had with our other two girls. I used every single one of those five days to maximize rest.

Moms are guilty of not resting when it comes to miscarriage too. Many of us feel we are not allowed the same space or time to recover. Our husbands don't get paternity leave. Many people don't even know what's going on because we look the same. Rushing our recovery, however, can lead to infection, medical issues and depression. I'm certainly an advocate of being strong, but know when you're choosing your pride to the detriment of your health.

If you are in a challenging health situation, lower your standards and prioritize your rest.

If you are going through something difficult, don't be afraid to ask for help. Sometimes when we're weak (physically or emotionally), it's hard for us to imagine that another mom has the strength to help us. Trust me, your friend, who isn't currently pregnant, can probably cook dinner for your family and drop it off.

Ask for help.

Let the people in your life who love you come and support you. Ask for food and babysitting help. Try to scare up some money to hire help with cleaning, watching the kids or cooking. Don't sacrifice your health by not resting.

You won't be able to keep managing your family and your home if you never recharge your batteries. You must take care of yourself if you're going to keep taking care of the people God has put in your life. Don't let pride keep you from the rest you need.

Chapter Five:
Finances

"If you would rise, shun luxury, for luxury lowers
and degrades."
— St John Chrysostom

It can be difficult to talk or even think about money. Sometimes we want to cover our ears, close our eyes, keep our head buried in the sand, and not think about money at all. But most of us don't have an endless supply of money, so we need to make and stick to a budget so we can be a good steward of the money God has given us.

You need to have a budget. You need to know where your money is going. What you spend your money on shows what you value. What are you valuing with your dollars? You also need to put how much you're spending into the context of your whole budget. If you are going out to eat with your spouse three times per week, you may call this "working on your marriage," but if you can't afford your water bill, it's not wise.

In addition to making a budget to help you manage your money going forward, it's also important to go back and review your bank statements for the last 12 months. Make a category for "eating out" and figure out how much you spent on that last year. Add up how many coffees you bought. How much are you spending on entertainment: cable, Netflix, going out to the movies, etc.

A budget is simply a spreadsheet where you're planning what you will be spending going forward and trying to stay within the numbers you've picked. Make sure it's an informed and educated guess based on your past spending. If you normally spend $200 per month on restaurants, creating a budget that gives you only $25 might be unrealistic. I'm all about cutting things out to focus on your financial plans, but make sure your plans are realistic.

Many of you don't have a budget and some of you are simply ignoring the budget you have. This is an unacceptable way to live. God wants us to be responsible with the money He has given us. We cannot keep spending our money on restaurants, movies, or new clothes, without saving for the future. This is absolutely a matter of faith. We cannot keep God and our finances in separate boxes.

If your household has two new cars, a $150 cable bill, two iPhones, and you're not tithing any money to your church, because "you can't afford it," you probably need to reevaluate your budget.

I'm a big fan of Dave Ramsey and *Financial Peace University*[29]. You can read about what he recommends on his website (www.daveramsey.com) but the basic idea is to create a budget, pay down all of your debt, and then cash flow all your purchases. We try to pay cash for everything we buy. Our goal is to be completely debt-free within ten years. The only loans we currently have are for our house and our business.

This didn't *just happen*. We don't go on vacation, we don't sign the kids up for expensive extracurricular activities, we buy most things used and we spend money within a tight budget we've created.

I'm not going to type out all of Dave Ramsey's program, but I think it's a great place to start. Go pick up his book[30], or sign up for a Financial Peace University session near you. He will help you figure out where to start and how to make baby steps toward financial freedom. Even if you're drowning, this is possible for you!

When things get tight, my husband and I go into "rice and beans" mode. This means we will spend absolutely no money on discretionary (fun and unnecessary) things and instead try to eat all the food in our cupboards to minimize our grocery bill. We do this until we are back on our feet. Maybe we needed repairs on the car, and our car fund wasn't big enough. Maybe we've decided to visit Michael's parents in Michigan, and we need to save money for that trip.

I really like www.mint.com, because it puts all my accounts into one place. I can see exactly where I'm spending my money. I also have a budget for the year which I break down monthly. It accounts for the money we spend on birthdays, hunting season, Christmas, trips, car maintenance, and money for books. It would be silly of me not to have a line item for books. I love buying books and, because we homeschool, we are constantly adding to our library. It would be irresponsible of me to not acknowledge that and plan for it.

We all have different financial situations. The important thing is that you are honest with yourself and your spouse about your situation. Don't stick your head in the sand. Pull out your bills and bank statements and create a budget based on how you actually live and what your financial goals are. Unchecked spending is irresponsible and is not a Godly way to live.

Be Honest With Yourself

"It is with the smallest brushes that the artist paints the
most exquisitely beautiful pictures."
– St. André Bessette

You do not need to live a big and glamorous lifestyle. Sit down and look at what you've spent your money on in the last six months. Maybe you've spent hundreds of dollars at Starbucks without realizing it. Maybe your credit card is so high that your interest payment alone is a couple hundred dollars a month now. Maybe you're spending $500 a month at Costco, and you justified that, because hey, you're only buying food, and you need to eat right?

Maybe you do have enough money that you really can spend $500 per month at Costco. Maybe you're feeding seven children with that budget! The important thing is that you don't hide from your financial situation. You need to own it, create a budget, and stick to your plan.

You need to be financially responsible with the resources God gave you. If your spouse is not willing to work on this with you, pray for them. I know that sounds like it's not enough. But if you're not at least doing that, start praying. Pray every single day that God changes the heart of your spouse so that the two of you can agree on a budget together.

It can be difficult to tell your husband what he can and can't spend his money on, especially if he is the one who is providing the primary income. God intended wives and husbands to work together. Spouses should honor each other with the money that they spend. This includes you. It's not okay to blow your family's money at the Nordstrom Anniversary Sale if you really can't afford it.

I'm probably not saying anything you don't know already. If you do not know how to make and manage a budget, you need to find a good resource. There are many websites and books that can help you with this.

Doing nothing is unacceptable. Not paying attention is only going to get you in trouble. You want to spend your money purposefully. That doesn't mean you can't ever have fun or buy frivolous things, but that needs to be part of your budget. Don't put your family into a dangerous situation by refusing to learn how to manage your finances.

Less Is More

*"Who except God can give you peace? Has the world ever
been able to satisfy the heart?"*
– Saint Gerard Majella

Most Americans would benefit by embracing minimalism. Less is more and most of us own too much stuff. Other than books, I have tried to get rid of most of my stuff. My kids don't have a lot of clothes. My closet doesn't have dozens of pairs of shoes. I use one purse for almost everything. We don't collect a lot of toys, and we rotate the ones that we have to keep them interesting. I try to buy things at consignment stores when possible. I shop clearance racks and sales when I need to buy something new.

This year I made a list of the Christmas gifts I wanted to buy, and I bought most of them at the Amazon Prime sale in July. Almost everything I wanted was deeply discounted, and now I have nearly all my presents while staying within my budget. My husband and I have been budgeting for five years, and we know to set aside money for presents. We buy them when they are on sale instead of grabbing high-priced items at the last minute. You may need to work on budgeting for a few months (or even years) before you can build up funds for these purposes.

In general, we buy one or two things for each child for their birthday. My husband and I don't exchange gifts very often. If you try this, don't set your husband up to fail here. You can't tell him that you're not doing presents for Christmas or your birthday but then be hurt and disappointed if he doesn't get you anything. You have to honor what you agree. If you can't handle not getting a present for Christmas from your husband, which isn't a terrible thing, then just give him a budget you want him to stay within.

My family and I don't buy presents for each other at Christmas. Grandparents buy something for the grandchildren. I do make a photo album and give that to all of the grandparents, because really, they don't need more things. They really just love seeing pictures of their family grow.

Don't get me wrong, I'm not trying to be Scrooge here. I certainly don't think buying presents is a bad thing. Many families can afford to do this, and giving presents is such a joyful activity! It just happens that most of my family are in a tight financial spot where they really can't afford to buy a lot of presents. Instead, we choose to spend time together and make memories, because that is how we express financial responsibility. Know what your family can afford and plan accordingly.

I really like the book *Clutter-Free With Kids*[31] by Joshua Becker. Unlike so many of the books about minimalism that are written by people with no children who live in big city condos and practice Eastern religions, Becker is a Christian and has children. He gives really great tips to balance minimalism with living in the real world, having children, and honoring Christ.

Finances Are Emotionally Draining

Working on your budget and saving money can be emotionally draining. It's important that while you're trying to get yourself out of a bad place, you don't tackle too many other things. It's probably not wise to cut back spending in most facets of your life while also trying to learn how to sew or lose thirty pounds. When it comes to creating your Weekly Plan, realize that financial changes will consume most of your willpower, leaving you with little left to improve other aspects of your life.

Try to break your financial plan into baby steps. Don't be overwhelmed by the $125,000 of student loans you have to pay off. Instead, try to think about saving just $1,000 to throw at the principal balance of your debt. I really like creating and filling in goofy thermometers so I have a visual motivator. It helps me appreciate the small steps along the way to my ultimate financial plan.

As with the other life facets, you will check in about your finances each week. You will adjust your plan and determine an appropriate next step - no more hiding your head in the sand. I want you to find financial freedom and financial peace.

Chapter Six:
Health

The Dalai Lama, when asked what surprised him most about humanity, said, "Man. Because he sacrifices his health in order to make money. Then he sacrifices money to recuperate his health. And then he is so anxious about the future that he does not enjoy the present; the result being that he does not live in the present or the future; he lives as if he is never going to die, and then dies having never really lived."

We know our health is important. I'm not going to waste time making a case for that. I think the better thing to talk about is why we continually put our health behind so many other areas of our life.

> Why do we think we can keep living off of Diet Coke and processed food and still be effective parents?
>
> Why don't we question our frequent headaches?
>
> Why have we just accepted the fact that we feel bloated and groggy most of the time?
>
> Why do we allow our busy life to keep us from taking care of the temple that God has given us?
>
> Why do we schedule annual check-ups for our children and let years go by without getting our own check-up?

I struggle with this facet of my life the most. I am a glutton for food; I am a stress eater; I really don't like to exercise; I don't like taking a shower, and I really don't feel like flossing my teeth ever. I forget to drink enough water. I like food that makes me sick, and I don't like food that makes me healthy.

I get it. Health is hard to prioritize.

It's not easy to focus on being healthy. Sometimes the idea of living a healthy life seems exhausting and expensive. I hide behind these excuses, or I tell myself I'll do it later when I'm not so busy. I'm really good at tricking myself into focusing on my marriage or my children when I don't feel like focusing on my health.

We have to stop lying to ourselves. We have to stop acting like petulant children who don't feel like eating our vegetables. If your body is broken and sick because of the choices you make, then you need to make better choices.

Living a healthy lifestyle will be different for each of us. I'm friends with several people who have autoimmune diseases, and my own mother has fibromyalgia. They will each have a different definition of what healthy means for them. If you are disabled in some way, or if your body is allergic to *everything*, don't wallow in your limitations. Acknowledge them, and plan accordingly.

My mom will never be what the world considers "healthy." Even in her limitations, however, she knows what things make her feel better and what things make her feel worse. She has a list of foods that she shouldn't eat, and she knows that she should be doing light exercise every single day. And when she deviates from her plan, her body hurts so badly that sometimes she can't even get out of bed.

You need to get to know your body and understand what healthy means for you. If you have never been taught what to eat, it's time to learn. I know there are countless diets, supplements, protein powders and meal plans out there. Don't be overwhelmed by all these choices.

Gluten may be good or bad. Who really knows? I've done hours of reading about it and I'm still not sure what to think. I do know, however, that eating pizza four nights a week is definitely bad. We don't need health books to understand that.

Here are some universal principles to start with:

- Eat more whole foods;
- Consume fewer processed foods;
- Cut down on refined sugar.

For me, it's not gluten that makes me sick. Rather I never seem to eat gluten without covering it in cheese or sugar and those make me sick. Pay attention to which foods make you feel poorly. Try to narrow down exactly which ones you have problems with and then cut them out. I want you to realize that your body is a temple of the Holy Spirit, who lives in you and was given to you by God!

> *"You do not belong to yourself, for God bought you with a*
> *high price. So you must honor God with your body."*
> *1 Corinthians 6:19-20*

God gave you your body. Take care of it. You only get one. There are no take-backs or exchanges. Love your body, because God gave it to you. Think of how we cherish certain spiritual items that have been blessed. We put them in a special place in our homes. We dust them and protect them. We wrap them carefully when we move and we never throw them away.

How much more then should we care for our bodies? God designed them for each of us uniquely.

Emotional and Mental Health Issues

"O Holy Spirit, descend plentifully into my heart.
Enlighten the dark corners of this neglected dwelling and
scatter there Thy cheerful beams."
— *St. Augustine*

No one likes to think that they have mental health problems. But our flesh is sinful, and humans tend to have addictive personalities. We want to feel good and satisfy the pleasures of the flesh. Sometimes the activities we engage in that are poor for our health stem from emotional issues and addictions.

It can be very difficult to make progress on your physical health, even if you're eating well and exercising if you're also dealing with an addiction. Whether you drink too much, you gamble, you're addicted to online shopping, you are an emotional eater, you're addicted to prescription painkillers, or you can't stop watching porn, you must acknowledge these issues if you're going to make progress.

Maybe you decide to drink more water to have a healthier lifestyle, but at the same time, you're still spending $400 per day on Amazon Prime. This is probably a disordered reaction. We need to deal with big fires before we deal with small ones. We need to ask ourselves what our worldly addictions are. What are the things or activities in your life you feel you couldn't live without?

One way to discover what your addictions are is to picture the activities you think you can't stop doing, even if you want to. That's how overeating feels for me. I know it's an addiction, because, even though I hate it and I don't want to do it, I compulsively do it anyway. Then I always feel terrible afterward.

In my booklet *A Catholic Guide To Overcome Emotional Eating,* I talk about how dieting doesn't fix the root of the problem when you are using food to soothe your emotions. The real problem is that you're using food instead of leaning on God. Cutting out sugar isn't going to solve this problem.

If you're clinically depressed, it's extremely difficult to make progress on your physical health. If you have a chemical imbalance in your body, you can't just "try harder" and tackle some of these other issues we're talking about. You need to see a doctor and you may need to go on some medication. I have had clinical depression twice in my life, and both times I needed to go on medication for a few months to stabilize myself so I could get healthier. Some people have to be on antidepressants for the rest of their lives.

Because I didn't want to consider myself depressed, I fought the idea of going to a doctor for a long time. My depression actually looked more like uncontrollable anger so it was harder to spot. I wasn't crying all the time, so I thought I was fine.

If you or someone you know suffers from clinical depression, this should not be a situation left up to prayer alone. Though I do believe that God can perform miracles, sometimes we really do just need some counseling and/or medication to get back on track. If you have a severe chemical imbalance in your body, perhaps your thyroid is not working correctly, you need medical help.

It can be hard to ask for help, but we must humble ourselves and do this for the sake of our families. Don't feel ashamed. God does indeed give us trials to endure, but we don't need to live through them without seeking out answers or help. Ask for people to pray for you, and go see a doctor.

Constant anger or anxiety can also cause our bodies to have physical health problems. If you suffer from worrying all the time or lashing out in anger at those around you, and you feel like you can't control either of these emotions, I would highly recommend reading some books on these topics.

God did not design our bodies to live in a constant state of anxiety and anger. These emotions break down our physical health.

> *"Because of your anger my whole body is sick; my health is broken because of my sins. My guilt overwhelms me – it is a burden too heavy to bear. My wounds fester in stink because of*

my foolish sins. I am bent over and racked with pain. My days are
filled with grief. A raging fever burns within me, and my health
is broken. I am exhausted and completely crushed. My groans
come from an anguished heart."
Psalms 38: 3-8

If you think that you are anxious or angry too often, don't despair.
There are many people who struggle with these emotions and,
thankfully, there are also many resources available to help. Don't be
afraid to ask for the help you need to get better.

Move Your Body

"The dress of the body should not discredit the good of the soul."
– St. Cyprian

There's a reason standing desks are becoming so popular. Americans spend too much time sitting. We need to move our bodies every single day. This applies to just about every person on the planet. Even my mom who has fibromyalgia, a disease which makes exercising painful, has instructions from her doctor to keep exercising. He says even though light exercise will be painful for her, her body will have less pain overall because of the health benefits of exercising.

It doesn't matter what you pick, just pick something. I really can't stand running. I like strength training in my bedroom. I use a kettle bell and my own body for weights. I do kettlebell swings, planks, squats, and push-ups. Then I go walking with my children. These things are easy and free, and I happen to enjoy them. I also like dance parties. Try putting on some good tunes and dancing for twenty minutes. It'll get your heart rate up, and your kids will love it!

If you like swimming, go swimming. If you like dancing, take a dance class. If you need group motivation, go to the gym and take a spin class. If you like the outdoors, go hiking.

Move your body. There's no excuse. You can find time to do it. If I can find fifteen minutes to get my heart rate up in my bedroom with three small children around, you can find something that works for you!

Be A Health Detective

*"Work hard every day at increasing your purity of heart,
which consists in appraising things and weighing them in
the balance of God's will."*
— *St. Francis de Sales*

If your body isn't working properly, stop and ask yourself why. Maybe you're not drinking enough water. Maybe you're allergic to something. Maybe you need to go to the doctor.

Don't be passive about your health. I have a friend that was having health problems and finally discovered that she shouldn't be eating FODMAPS[32]. It turns out there's a whole list of foods that people who can't have FODMAPS shouldn't eat including berries, apples, onions, yogurt, honey, and beer! Knowing *not* to eat these foods is not intuitive. Once she followed the FODMAP diet, she felt great!

It took my husband a long time to find out he was mildly allergic to peppers. He was eating breakfast sausage that had peppers in them, and he was having problems. The important thing is that he didn't just accept that his body wasn't working well. He kept taking out certain foods and putting certain foods back in until he figured out what was the source of his issues.

Take a deep breath. Drink more water, because really, we all need more water than we're drinking. Then listen to your body. Our bodies are a masterpiece that God designed, most of them can give us the feedback we need to figure out what's going wrong.

I have another friend who has a disease where her body thinks she has hepatitis, even though it doesn't, and so it attacks her fake hepatitis and causes problems. That is a unique situation. Most people aren't going to experience this. My friend, who is going through this very confusing health situation, is still committed to figuring something out. Although it would be easy, she doesn't simply give up and say, "Oh well, I guess this is just how I am."

Be your own health detective and figure out what makes your body work well, then do that. Later you're going to create your own Catholic Mom Manifesto and, in that, you will write down a list of things that help you to be healthy and a list of things that make you feel bad. This will be a quick place you can look to help you stay on track with your health plan.

Chapter Seven:
Homemaking

"This, in short, is the difference between us and others
who know not God, that in misfortune they complain and
murmur, while the adversity does not call us away from
the truth of virtue and faith, but strengthens us
by its suffering."
–St. Cyprian

It's quite ridiculous to me when I think about writing anything on the topic of homemaking. I grew up in a small apartment with a single mother who didn't make me do anything. I think she felt so badly about our family situation that she didn't want us to feel worse by doing chores.

By the time I went to college, I knew how to cook a few things, but I certainly didn't know how to manage or clean a household. I have also never cared that much about things being tidy or clean. I made sure my laundry was clean but it didn't bother me if it was in a pile on the floor.

Learning how to value a clean and tidy household was something I had to learn after I got married and became a mother.

It was actually a very painful experience for me to become a stay-at-home mom. I realized that I had no skills related to that vocation. I studied finance in college. I was a certified dog trainer. I knew how to build websites and help small businesses write business plans. But I didn't know how often you should change your sheets, what you should use to clean your floors, or how to take care of a backyard.

It was embarrassing and very demoralizing. Not being good at my new "job" was one of the things that led me to a dark place, including depression, in the first years of my marriage. It felt really awful to not use the skills I had and to be in charge of a bunch of things I didn't know how to do.

Eventually, and with the help of the Catholic Mom Challenge, I got to the place where I just admitted that I was very bad at my job. I knew I was going to be a homemaker for a long time. If I wanted to stop feeling sorry for myself, then I needed to go and learn how to be a good homemaker.

Embrace Being A Homemaker

*"He who can preserve gentleness amid pains, and peace
amid worry multitude of affairs, is almost perfect."*
–St. Francis de Sales

I really like the term "homemaker," and I think we don't use it often enough. Even if you're a working mom, it's likely that you're the one in charge of what goes on in your house. You "make" the house into the home that it is. You probably choose how it is decorated. You probably do the grocery shopping and the cooking. You probably do the laundry yourself or poke others in your family to get it done. It's good that we think of ourselves as homemakers.

We are making a home out of the place we live in, whether it's a one bedroom apartment or a mansion on a lake.

In addition to wanting to be better about cleaning my house and creating systems to help things run smoothly, I also wanted to create an atmosphere of peace for my children, my husband, and my guests. I read about this concept in Katie Warner's book *Head and Heart: Becoming Spiritual Leaders of Your Family.*[33] It really hit me as such a powerful idea, both as a mother and especially as a spiritual leader in my family, it is my job to cultivate an atmosphere of peace in our home.

The idea of cultivating peace and being a spiritual leader in my household is so much more attractive to me than just thinking about creating a chore schedule. We do use a chore schedule as one of the tools to help us achieve an atmosphere of peace in our house, but this idea gives the chore schedule a deeper meaning for me.

If you're not sure where to begin, ask yourself what do you *not* know? What skills do you need to acquire to be better in this area? Stop lying to yourself and making excuses. Commit yourself to being better.

I'm all about tough love, but don't be too hard on yourself either. You shouldn't feel really guilty about not having a perfectly clean and organized home. It took me years to get to the place where I had a functioning system for homemaking, and it's always evolving. Some moms can get too caught up in wanting things to be perfect. Don't sacrifice your faith or having carefree timelessness with your family by being too focused on cleaning the house. There is always a balance.

When I have a really busy day filled with homeschooling, grocery shopping, and delivering a meal to a new mom, I don't beat myself up about not cleaning the bathrooms.

By contrast, some days I wake up late, lie around in my jammies all day, and spend collectively two hours (in five-minute bursts) scrolling through my phone. When I get to the end of those days and realize I didn't clean the bathrooms, it's a lie for me to say, "Life with little kids is just so hard. It's impossible to get anything done!"

We have to examine our own lives truthfully, one day at a time.

Create Systems

Running a house smoothly requires staying on top of many different tasks. You can group these tasks by room, you can group these tasks by the tools you use to complete them, or you can group these tasks by the frequency you perform them. Create a system to tackle all the different aspects of managing your home. Where possible, group like tasks together.

One of my favorite concepts that I use in homemaking is the idea of using "loops." I first read about loops on Sarah Mackenzie's blog *Amongst Lovely Things*.[34] She described using loops in her homeschool schedule. A loop is simply a list of the things you want to be done. Instead of assigning a schedule to these tasks, however, you simply move from one task to the next, as you have time.

If you don't finish a particular task by the end of the day, you start with that task tomorrow, then continue moving down the list. Instead of doing laundry on Mondays and bathrooms on Tuesdays, your list might say laundry, bathrooms, kitchen floors, and backyard clean-up. If you happen to do laundry on Tuesday, then bathrooms are up next. You might slam out both those things in one day. Alternatively, if you are in the middle of a baseball tournament, you might delay the next item on the list until Saturday.

I use a blend of scheduling and loops. There are some activities I do based on the day of the week (i.e. laundry on Mondays and Thursdays, floors on Tuesday, bathrooms on Friday etc.) Then I put some of the more specialized housekeeping items on a loop list (i.e. wipe down kitchen cupboards, clean out the laundry room, reorganize my closet etc.) When I have some free time, I can pull out my loop list and simply do the next item on the list.

There are many books and websites dedicated to teaching you how to organize your home, create a housekeeping schedule, and build a meal plan. Find a system that works for you. Be a scientist and check in often to see if you like it. You might need to keep trying until you find one that fits your personality and temperament.

We'll talk about willpower later in this book as a finite resource that runs out. You want to put as many decisions on autopilot as you can so you're not using mental energy to decide what to do next. Having a schedule, a loop, or some other system will simplify your decision. You won't have to constantly be asking yourself what to do next. You simply refer to your list or system to discover your task and then complete it.

Survival Mode

I have a friend who has three kids under five, and one of them has special needs. On top of that, her husband works twelve-hour shifts, so she is basically a single mom for many days out of the week. She's in a very difficult season of life right now, and I would never look at her and say, "Why don't you just make a cleaning schedule and stick to it?"

Sometimes you really are just in survival mode. Be reasonable.

If this is true for you right now, just be honest with yourself. Tell yourself you're in survival mode. Make a list of the minimum you need to do. Then let the rest go. Don't feel guilty about the other stuff. Screaming at your family does real damage, right now. Love God, love your spouse, love your children and most of the rest of it can wait.

When I'm in survival mode, I know we need frozen veggies in the freezer, and I have to make sure everyone has clean underwear. I also make sure there is no mold growing in the toilets - at least right before anyone shows up to visit! That may sound awful, but that's how I maintain my sanity in survival mode.

God does not want us to be anxious. He did not design our human bodies to handle prolonged, high levels of stress. Being anxious makes our bodies physically sick. Don't give in to it.

You can also find tips and recommendations in the Catholic Mom Challenge Facebook group[35]. There are lots of seasoned ladies out there who have great advice for creating systems that work in the home.

Now that we've talked a little bit about the seven facets we're responsible for, let's move on and talk about how the Catholic Mom Challenge system can help us manage those facets in a more organized, peaceful and God-centered way.

Part Two:

The Catholic Mom Challenge System

The Catholic Mom Challenge System

*"Let us thank God for having called us to His holy faith.
It is a great gift, and the number of those who thank God
for it is small."*
— *St. Alphonsus Liguori*

The older I get, the more I think, "We live in some really scary times." Then I wonder, maybe most people feel this way as they get older and see more evil in the world. Whether we perceive this darkness or not, evil is very real. I believe Catholic moms have the power, by raising faithful children who love Christ, to create light in the world and repel the growing darkness.

Until Jesus returns, we will always have sadness, poverty, war, and political strife. Our aim is not to get rid of these issues – they will always exist. In the living room of our domestic church, however, we can sway the tide. We can keep the world from slipping further into darkness and we can try to heal the pain that exists.

We have the power to raise an entire generation of people who love Christ and are His hands in the world. Imagine if all of us focused less on getting our children into college and more on creating saints.

Of course, college is important. You don't need to give that up, but so many of us have chosen to teach our children to achieve worldly accolades instead of raising them to live deeply faithful lives. So many of us have chosen to focus on the growth of our children while letting our own faith grow stagnant. We should be striving for sainthood, and the more effective we are in this aim, the more our children will desire this for themselves as well.

What an amazing work we could accomplish in just forty years if we raised engaged Catholic children who then raised more deeply Catholic children! The work you do is important. Catholic moms are incredibly powerful. We may not feel like it when we are cleaning spaghetti off the floor, being stonewalled by our teenager, folding laundry, or reading Dr. Seuss books for the thousandth time, but we are. You are important and powerful. You were made to become a saint.

Striving For Sainthood

"We know certainly that our God calls us to a holy life.
We know that he gives us every grace, every abundant
grace; and though we are so weak of ourselves, this grace
is able to carry us through every obstacle and difficulty."
— *St. Elizabeth Ann Seton*

The Catholic Mom Challenge is about striving for sainthood. It's about becoming the holiest person you could possibly become. This is possible for you, mama, I promise. God created us so we could be sanctified. That's why we should study the lives of the saints: so we can see how thousands of ordinary people were able to achieve this.

When you make sainthood your aim, you will lead those around you to sainthood, as well. People are attracted to holiness. They will want the peace you have. Your husband will become more holy; your children will become more holy, and your neighbors will notice how brightly your light shines in the world. They will want to know why.

This is not too good to be true. This is how God's economy works. It doesn't always happen right away. You may not even see the lives you touch as you strive for sainthood. Some people may choose Christ only with their very last breath. You must strive for sainthood even if you don't see any fruits of your journey until you reach Heaven.

Striving for sainthood doesn't always look grand. For some of you, the path to sainthood will involve being a prayer warrior for the rest of your life. God may simply be asking you to pray for your family and the world every single day until you die. Though this may seem too easy, having the faith to do this every day can be quite difficult. Sainthood may be achieved in very simple ways, but it is never easy.

I wanted to create and share the Catholic Mom Challenge system to help my fellow Catholic mamas to have more peace. I want us to stop living with fear and anxiety. I want us to get our focus off the shiny worldly things that we don't need and instead to fix our eyes on Christ.

Another way to say this is that I want all Catholic moms to become saints in Heaven. I believe our entire purpose here on Earth is to strive for sainthood. Our path to sainthood will be unique but our aim should be the same.

Goals are For Losers

You might expect me to talk a lot about goals. This is not a program about setting goals. After reading *How To Fail At Almost Everything and Still Win Big* by Scott Adams,[36] I changed the way I thought about goals.

Adams says that goals are for losers, adding "Let's say you want to lose ten pounds, so every day you weigh yourself and you're like, 'Eh, I'm failing' even if you're getting closer. You're in this pre-success, kind of semi-failure, purgatory, emotional state. You're not feeling like you're a success."[37]

When you set a goal and check in with that goal, most of the time you will have failed at achieving it, even if you're making progress. We carry these feelings of failure along our journey. Our brains are noting failure instead of success even if we're making progress. I don't want this for you. I want you to feel successful along the way as you strive for sainthood.

While I'm not going to advocate throwing it out of the English language, I want you to change the way you think about the word "goals." We need to stop viewing "goals" as an objective and more as a process. We're not going to focus on goals in this program.

Instead, we are going to instill habits and create systems to achieve our mission. It's okay to have goals but I want you to translate them into discrete habits and tasks you're going to tackle.

We will examine each of the six facets of life and try to discern what God's purpose is for that facet. This will be our mission, and we will create habits and systems to help us aim for our mission. We will be reviewing how things are going weekly, monthly, quarterly and annually, and we will adjust our aim if we need to.

We're going to do this with Jesus. We're going to spend our lives soaking up Christ's love and striving for sainthood. That is our aim.

St. Francis de Sales describes the importance of always assessing our situation and adjusting our aim.

> *"Anxiety is a temptation in itself and also the source from and by which other temptations come. Therefore, above all else, be calm and compose your mind. Gently and quietly pursue your aim."*
>
> *St Francis de Sales*

God's Sense of Humor

Before we dive into the system, I have to share a story with you. It's the kind of story that helps you see how very little control we have over our own lives. This is especially appropriate to understand when you're about to go through a program that will teach you to get more control over your life.

Let me take you back to March of 2015.

My family was living in Hillsboro, OR. I had a five-year-old, a two-and-a-half-year-old and I was five months pregnant. At this point in our lives, we were feeling settled in our tiny home. We had a future goal of moving to a smaller city in three to five years. We had talked about Bend, Oregon or Boulder, Colorado or maybe some small town we hadn't even discovered yet. My husband loves the country, and we wanted to move away from the noise, traffic, and the crumbling values of the city of Portland.

Suddenly, the company my husband worked for announced a Voluntary Severance Package program. They basically said, "We'll give you several months of your salary if you leave."

At first, we said, "Well that's crazy, we couldn't possibly do that."

But as days passed, I noticed my heart softening to the idea. Could we do it? Could we leave this very stable job and move right now? I would ponder these things while softly rubbing my growing tummy. I took it to prayer and gave it to Jesus. *Thy will be done Lord; show me what you want.*

In a series of events, my husband and I both felt that God clearly pointed us in the direction of moving to Boise, Idaho. We had friends who called and told us about a job opportunity my husband might be interested in. I was reading Sherry Weddell's book *Forming Intentional Disciples,*[38] where she talked about the thriving Catholic community in Boise. My husband heard Boise's praises being sung on a national Catholic podcast he was listening to. Finally, the bi-annual Catholic women's conference in Boise just happened to be two weeks away. It only happened every two years and there it was, right around the corner!

I was still skeptical and emotional, as most pregnant women tend to be. I said a lot of things like, "We already had Boise in our minds, so we were just looking for signs. How do we know if this is God's will or our own?"

My husband would say, "Let's keep praying about it, and God will show us."

I decided to keep my heart open. I left my two girls with my husband and drove, by myself, for seven hours to that women's conference in Boise. If ever there was a place where I could get a good pulse on the Catholic community, it seemed like it would be this conference. And like a crazy person, I even took a map with me and asked anyone who would talk to me, where they lived and how they liked Boise. We had been living in a neighborhood with almost no children and zero Catholics, so that was one of the big things I was hoping to change if we moved.

Much to my surprise, I wasn't thrown out of the conference for being nosy. Rather, I was greeted with warm smiles and open hearts who shared with me how much they loved the city and thought it was a wonderful place to raise children. And yes, they even showed me where they lived and which neighborhoods were filled with children! I met some pretty wonderful homeschooling moms, too, who gave me hope that this really could be the place for us.

The conference happened to be the day before Divine Mercy Sunday. I have a deep devotion to St. Faustina and Divine Mercy, so it was a particularly special Sunday for me. As I was driving home, I prayed to Jesus, "Please, help me to know your will for us."

One more important detail of the story is that my mom's fibromyalgia had gotten so bad that she had to stop working. She and her husband were struggling financially and needed to move in with us. At this point, though, they didn't have any other options. They were both very against moving to Boise. They didn't want to leave their friends and family in Portland. I had been feeling pressured not to move so I could stay and take care of them.

As I drove home, on Divine Mercy Sunday, I finished praying the Divine Mercy chaplet in the car. I did something I almost never do. I asked God for a sign. I'm pretty hesitant to ever ask for this. I have this idea that I should have enough faith to not need miraculous signs. I was emotionally drained, completely confused, and I genuinely did just want to do what God wanted me to do. I let the silence hang in the car as I drove through the beautiful foothills of Idaho.

Just then, my phone rang. It was my mother, and she said, "Honey, I love you. I just wanted to call and say that if you and Michael move to Boise, we will come with you." She sounded so peaceful when she said it, and that's when I knew. We were going.

Everything Is Going to Be Fine

We often have this idea that, when we are doing something beautiful and noble for Jesus, He will open all the right doors and smooth the way. Because I was so confident I was following His will, I expected everything about the move to fall into place.

It did not.

There were lots of bumps in the road. Oh, the bumps! I ended up having a pinched nerve in my back because the baby was sitting too low. I could barely walk or bend over for the last six weeks of my pregnancy, which included packing and moving. We had to live out of an apartment for a month in ninety-plus degree weather while we were looking for a house, so we basically had to move twice.

There were many shenanigans before finally finding a house we could buy. We had to make a mad dash for appliances when the previous owners decided to keep theirs at the last minute. *Don't tell a pregnant lady she has no refrigerator or washer!* And finally, we had one serious false start to having the baby the day after we got the keys to our house.

It was a whirlwind time that lasted two months, but we made it. We were happily nestled in Boise, Idaho, finally a family of five plus two grandparents.

I thought everything was going to be great.

After one month of working, my husband came home one day and said, "This isn't the job for me."

My heart sank. Here I was with a new baby, in a new city - and a much smaller city where you can't just find another job at the drop of a hat - and I saw this awful sadness in his eyes. I know many husbands make the great sacrifice of going to a job they don't like to support the family they love. I knew he would do that for us if I asked him. At the same time, however, I loved him so much that I didn't want him having to endure a yucky environment for eight-plus hours a day.

The next day, I sat down at my computer and Googled "Boise business for sale." It was the only thing I could think of. A few months later, stunned and totally unprepared for what was ahead of us, we bought Heartland Post & Pole, an agricultural fence manufacturing and installation company.

Here is the crucial part of this story. Up until that time, I had been a stay-at-home mom, albeit perhaps a grumpy, slightly unsatisfied stay-at-home mom, but that's what I was. Spending all day with three tiny humans can really test your sanity, and it's no easy job, but it was my job - and largely my identity.

When we bought Heartland, we had this idea that my mom would watch my kids for four hours in the middle of the day and I would do bookkeeping, handle phone calls and do fence bids for the company. It sounded like a nice hybrid. I'd have a small break from the kids; I could help the company; and my mom, who could no longer work, could help me out with the kids. It actually sounded kind of fun to me!

It wasn't fun. It was awful.

There's no other way to say it. There weren't four hours of work to do every day, there were ten. I couldn't compartmentalize the work like I had intended. The phone rang all day, sometimes forty times in a single day! I was constantly interrupted when I was with the kids, asking them to be quiet or go in another room. Our homeschool schedule was destroyed. The kids started watching Netflix every day when, previously, we had only done this as a special treat on Sundays.

We started eating a lot of hot dogs and – gasp – gluten. When the going gets tough, Paleo home cooking is hard to pull off. I brought store-bought food to any event we were invited to. Look, I know that's a stupid thing to even mention, but when you identify yourself as a home cooking, healthy food mama, it feels like a big deal!

For those of you who follow my blog or listen to my Coffee & Pearls podcast, my publications stopped coming out every Tuesday. I gained fifteen pounds in three months despite my previous plan to lose fifteen pounds in those same three months. I was losing my grip on all of my systems and on my own sanity. I felt like I had lost my identity and compromised all the truly important things in my life: my health, my family, and even my faith. I started to feel like God had left me alone in this darkness.

I went to Adoration one night. I didn't even make it into the chapel because I knew what I really needed to do was ugly-cry in front of Jesus. I settled for sitting in my car, in front of the chapel, sobbing my eyes out and saying all the things out loud - and loudly - that I needed to say to my Abba Father.

Why has this happened to me? I was just trying to help my husband and my parents. I can't handle everything you've asked me to be responsible for. I've been praying, Lord give me strength, and you're not there! What am I supposed to do? Who am I supposed to be?

Soon my questions turned into confessions.

I've been a terrible mother and a grumpy wife. I feel awful about myself. I'm soothing myself with food instead of you. I feel hopeless. I don't know what to do. I don't know how to cope. I want to spend my life teaching women how to manage their lives, and here I've crashed and burned in my own. I'm so ashamed and embarrassed. I don't know where to start.

Lord, help me.

I vented all the hurt, the bitterness, the sadness, the hopelessness, and the grief. I was mourning the life I thought I was going to have - being a balanced Catholic, healthy, homeschooling, blogging wife and mother.

Here's the point in the story where I'd love to say that I heard angelic voices telling me – anything – but I didn't. I heard nothing as I sat there in the car…coming down… feeling the weight of all that I confessed to both Jesus and myself.

The only feeling I had inside of me seemed to say, "You're not ready."

I wasn't ready. I felt like there was something I was waiting for. Perhaps something I needed to learn or needed to do. I did the only thing I knew how to do. I kept on living and kept on praying. I never stopped praying, though I had let my daily Bible reading slip. I decided to put Bible reading back in and to up my prayer time.

In the end, this is what we should always choose. Every day we wake up, God has decided that we should be alive, which means we should thank Him and pray. No matter what you're going through, this is true for you today. Thank God for being alive today.

I clung to this because it was the only thing I felt certain of.

Three months later, out of the blue, my husband's new company also offered a Voluntary Severance Package. My husband took it and left one week later. Without any ideas about how we were going to tackle our life, we felt confident this was the right choice for us. We could afford for him to take four months off while he helped me with Heartland and before he would need to find another job.

When this book is published, he will be two months into this time.

Ladies, I share this with you because I genuinely believe God put me in this crazy, whirlwind, unpredictable six months so that I would completely overhaul this program. Last year, I think my program would have sounded a lot like this:

You should go to Adoration weekly. You have the time; make it a priority.

And that wouldn't have been terrible advice, but now I know what it's like to be so caught up in a tornado of stress and activities and demands that are out of your control, that it feels like going to Adoration once a week *is* impossible.

When you read this book, I want you to understand that, not only do I know what it's like to feel like you're drowning, but that is precisely the time I forged this program. I took my original CMC program and, after picking up the crumpled version off the floor, I looked at it again.

Is it possible? Could I really create a system that would work? How can I help someone who feels as if they're underwater?

How could I give hope to the hopeless? And at the time, I did feel hopeless. Let's dive into the program, and I'll tell you what finally helped me get a grip.

Chapter Eight:
Getting Started

"Pray, hope, and don't worry."
-St. Padre Pio

These next sections of the book will give you an overview of the system. I recommend you read all the steps before you dive in. All the worksheets can be found at www.catholicmomchallenge.com. You can choose to print them out first if you want to have them in front of you as I describe each one.

I long for organization because I want to be in control of my own life. I believe if I can stay on top of everything, plan enough, schedule properly, create enough to-do lists, and design enough systems, then things will go the way I want – or at least the way I predict they will go. We all know this is impossible to achieve, yet we continue to seek control in these ways. Not only are we *not in control* of our lives, but being anxious about everything reveals our lack of trust in God.

Hyper-control robs us of our peace.

While it's reasonable to make plans and think things through, it's not okay to lose your mind when things go awry. God already has a great plan for your life, even though you can't see it. I guarantee you that, if you woke up this morning, God wants to use you in some way for great good. Take a deep breath and try to find some peace in that idea.

The God of the universe loves you and willed you into being so you could exist at this very moment. He has a plan for your life, but this doesn't mean you should sit at home and wait for something to happen to you. We still have to make responsible choices like creating grocery lists and family budgets.

Within our lives, we must still seek to bring some sense of organization and order to what we can. It's dangerous to get too emotionally wrapped up in *our* plans, or feel frustrated with ourselves and those around us when things don't go as we expected.

The Catholic Mom Challenge system will help you to take a deep breath, get in tune with God, and be honest with yourself. You will evaluate each area of your life so you can make a realistic plan going forward. Let's take a look at the steps you'll go through.

First, I'm going to give you a high-level overview of the Catholic Mom Challenge system. Don't be overwhelmed by the number of steps. Most of them go quite quickly, and many of them you only do the very first time you make your Catholic Mom Manifesto. Then I will break down each of the steps in more detail. The instructions will also be included in each of the worksheets that you will fill out.

Initial CMC Planning Session

Here are the steps you will go through the very first time you go through the Catholic Mom Challenge program. Start by scheduling your planning session. I think two hours is a good amount of time. I like to start my planning session in Adoration, if possible.

1. Get in tune with God (confession, adoration, prayer etc.)
2. Fill out Life Planning worksheets
3. Fill out the Annual Planning worksheets
4. Fill out your Monthly Plan and Weekly plan worksheets
5. Create your Catholic Mom Manifesto
6. Go out and tackle life!

Your Catholic Mom Manifesto won't change often. This little booklet will have all your stewardship statements, your mission statements, tips for success, obstacles to look out for, and quotes to help anchor you to Christ in times of stress. This little booklet is a lifesaver. I keep it with me in my purse and I review it at least once a day. It's an integral part of the Catholic Mom Challenge system.

Your Catholic Mom Manifesto will be a reminder of what you have decided is important to you. You will go through planning sessions annually, quarterly, monthly and weekly.

Every time you sit down to have a planning session, you will go through five steps.

Chapter Nine:
The Five Planning Steps

Here's a snapshot of the steps you'll go through when you're in a planning session.

1. Get in tune with God
2. Review your stewardship and mission statements
3. Assess where you are at
4. Review and adjust your aim
5. Create a plan and move forward

This is the process I'm going to teach you. We will do this in-depth once a year. We will review and adjust our aim once a quarter and once per month. Then, we will do a quick version of these steps every week. I know you're busy, so the quick part is important!

This system is designed to be easy and straightforward. I want to help you cut out the fluff and give you a clear focus on what's important. By embracing your Catholic faith and striving for sainthood, your life is going to get a lot simpler. It won't necessarily become easier, but my hope is that I can help you minimize your anxiety, your confusion, and the amount of time you waste worrying about or chasing after the wrong things.

When we declutter our homes, our minds, and our hearts, we find more peace in our souls.

Get In Tune With God

"Pray as though everything depended on God. Work as
though everything depended on you."
-St. Augustine[39]

As I mentioned before, we're going to focus on six facets of your life.
Each of those facets sits on a foundation of faith. Faith is the other side
of the circle. Your spirituality is always going to be part of everything
you do, and it should guide every decision you make. You may have
other, more urgent items on your to-do list, but your faith and striving
for sainthood should be like a mist around you that affects everyone
you interact with and any task you tackle.

No matter how you're spending your time, continually ask yourself,
"Is this pleasing to my Father in Heaven?"

If you find yourself thinking, "How can I know the will of God? How
do I know if something pleases Him?" then you're not alone in asking
this question. I have often felt as if the Lord is far from me, and when I
ask questions, all I seem to get back is silence. After all, most of us will
spend our entire lives without ever hearing the direct voice of God or
seeing visions of angels or Mary.

There are things you can do to tune into God even if you never hear
His voice out loud.

First, you have to give God the chance to speak with you. You need to
spend time in prayer every day and go to Adoration regularly. You
need to go to Mass. You need to go to Confession, monthly if possible.
You need to read your Bible daily. Sit down and pray a rosary or the
Divine Mercy Chaplet. These activities will help get your heart in tune
with God. Then, from this place of peace and spiritual rest, you can
close your eyes, sit quietly, and just listen.

Grab a piece of paper and start writing what comes to mind. God
whispers things into our hearts. I know when God does this because I'll
hear myself thinking of an idea that wouldn't have come from me.
Sometimes they're even things I really don't want to do, then I

especially know God is poking me! Don't judge what you're thinking, just start writing.

Write down everything that comes to mind. Then keep praying. Ask God for wisdom. Ask God for guidance. Ask God to help you discern what His plan is for your life. Give yourself the time and space to listen. Really give yourself over to Him.

Eventually, you will find nuggets of truth in your stream of consciousness writing. You'll start to set aside your worries and concerns, and you'll see a theme or a specific action pop up. I do this exercise often and it helps give me the clarity to write down all my thoughts. Committing them to paper helps me to identify when I'm just in a crazy, worried, and complaining mood. It allows me to calm down and become more reasonable.

Don't stop there, though. Sometimes we get so caught up in wanting things from the Lord that we forget to spend time just loving Him. When we love someone, we spend time with them. We want to make them happy. Don't just ask God for favors, really love Him. Love Him with your time. Love Him by giving Him space to talk to you. I have this quote from St. Thomas Aquinas in my Catholic Mom Manifesto to remind me of this very idea:

"To love God is something greater than to know Him." -
St. Thomas Aquinas

Love is not something we do from afar. Get up close and personal with our Lord, not just because you want Him to help you, but simply because you are trying to love Him. Start thinking of God as a friend who you want to get to know better. Spend time with Him to learn from Him. Spend time with Him simply to love Him.

In addition to the weekly and monthly time I spend with God trying to adore Him, I also involve Him in all my planning sessions. I take about two hours to get in tune with God (usually in Adoration,) and I go to Confession before sitting down to do my Annual Planning exercises.

I take one hour to be with the Lord before reviewing and adjusting my quarterly plans. I also try to make sure my quarterly planning session comes after I go to Confession, which is ideally on the first Saturday of the month.

I take twenty minutes to get in tune with God during Adoration once per week when I'm reviewing the week and planning the next week. Sometimes, life gets in the way and I do it in my living room instead. Don't let the perfect situation get in the way of getting your planning done!

Ask yourself right now, how much time are you spending with God?

If you're feeling particularly stressed or confused, could it be related to the distance you've put between yourself and Jesus? Often, when I'm in a dark place, I'll look back and realize I've spent less than one whole hour with Him the entire week! How are we supposed to be in tune with the God of the universe if we are ignoring Him one hundred and sixty-seven hours per week?

When I'm feeling sassy, I like to call this step, "Check yo self before you wreck yo self."

You *need* daily prayer time and you need to spend time with the Lord. You need to have an actual relationship with Him. Letting God slip into the background will only bring you confusion and loneliness. He is there, always waiting for you. He is so pleased when you turn to Him. He will always have His arms open wide, ready to embrace you, no matter what you do.

Keep reading through the rest of the steps, then I'll cover how we tackle the Annual Planning exercises. It doesn't matter if it's January, September, or another time of the year; anytime is a great time to take charge of your life.

Stewardship and Mission Statements

*"I urge you to remain steadfast in faith so that at last we
will all reach heaven and there rejoice together."*
— *St. Andrew Kim Taegon*

The first exercise you will go through in the Catholic Mom Challenge is
to write out your Stewardship Statements and your Mission
Statements:

> **Stewardship Statements** describe the people, causes and things
> that God has already put in your life and asked you to care for.

> **Mission Statements** describe the best-version-of-yourself that
> you want to become.

You will write one Stewardship Statement and one Mission Statement
for each facet of your life. While Stewardship Statements focus on your
current reality, Mission Statements guide you toward the ideal version
of yourself. Stewardship statements are about responsibilities that you
already have. Mission Statements paint a picture of your future and
perfect self that you will always be striving for.

As we become better stewards and get closer to fulfilling our mission,
we become more sanctified. You want to be a saint. That is your aim.
The statements are the guideposts along the way.

We have already talked about how each of us should be striving for
sainthood. The ultimate prize is to have lived our life in such a way
that when we get to heaven, Jesus says, "Well done, my good and
faithful servant." Matthew 25:21 Close your eyes and actually picture
what that moment would feel like.

I'll be honest, it's hard for me to think that I will ever be worthy of this.
The more I read about the life of Christ and the lives of the saints, the
more I see my own sin and how it keeps me far from my Father.

At the same time, I believe that His mercy is endless and that I can
continue to throw myself at the foot of the Cross. I ask for His
forgiveness over and over again. It is important that we continue to

uphold this image in our minds as the ultimate prize. We must seek out all the things that keep us from attaining sainthood and cut them out. This will be an ongoing process that we have to go through for the rest of our time on Earth.

So you already know your main mission is to become a saint in heaven. Now we must figure out what your sub-missions are. What are all the unique ways that you are going to achieve sainthood? The first thing you're going to do is to write out all the things God has asked you to be a steward of.

Stewardship Statements

"None of us is alone in this world. Each of us is a vital piece of the great mosaic of humanity as a whole."
–St. John Paul II

God has deliberately put certain people, things, and opportunities in your path. Later, you will write down what comes to mind for each of the life facets. Everything you list in each of the facets plays a role in how God is asking you to become a saint.

When you get up in the morning and you ask yourself, "Why am I here?" these statements will answer that question. You can look at your Marriage Stewardship statement and remember that God has asked you to care for your spouse and to try to get your spouse to Heaven. I know it can be helpful for me to read this when I'm feeling frustrated about the little things Michael does that annoy me. It helps put our relationship in perspective and helps me focus on what really matters.

It's easy for us to get disconnected – what does cleaning my house have to do with Jesus? Is drinking a healthy amount of water each day really going to help get me to Heaven?

Stewardship statements are the key to helping us make connections from our everyday lives to our ultimate goal of becoming a saint.

You can create more efficient routines, follow a tight budget, and even schedule your religious activities, but without understanding why you're doing these things, it's likely you'll run out of steam and fail to keep these plans. We often say that we are motivated to make money or save time. But in the end, we won't have any money, our bodies will decay in the ground, and we will have run out of time here on Earth. Ultimately, these things don't matter.

Achieving sainthood is the end. It's what we all want to accomplish with our lives. God has already given you glimpses of the type of saint you can be. If you have a child with a disability, she is likely a big key to your sainthood. If your family lives in a third world country to share the gospel, that is likely the key to your sainthood. If you have an ordinary family in the United States and you teach your ordinary children to love Jesus, that may be your key to sainthood.

I don't want you to think your path to sainthood has to be filled with superhuman things. Even the very simple things God asks us to do can be overwhelmingly difficult. We don't need to climb mountains to prove our love for Him. Sometimes our great task is to simply love those in our own home. I love this quote from G.K. Chesterton. It underlines the idea that simply living our lives with love can be amazing.

> *"The most extraordinary thing in the world is an ordinary man and an ordinary woman and their ordinary children." G.K. Chesterton*[40]

God has put very specific people and situations into your path. These are meant to forge you into a saint. For me, taking care of my young parents is part of my path to sainthood. This is probably also part of my husband's path to sainthood, too!

You have the opportunity to grow more and more like Jesus in the life you have right in front of you. You don't need to accomplish great things in order to become the best-version-of-yourself. You just need to take small steps and do the next right thing as often as you can.

The stewardship statement is about acknowledging what God has already asked you to take care of. Then you can ask yourself, "Am I doing a good job?" Maybe God hasn't answered some of your prayers asking Him for more because you aren't yet taking care of what He has already given you.

Here are some examples of my stewardship statements.

Example: Marriage Stewardship:

God has entrusted Michael Jaquith to me as my husband. My job is to love him, respect him, and to lead him to Heaven. It is my responsibility to show a good example of marriage to my children. God has called me to use my marriage as an example of God's love in the world.

Example: Health Stewardship:

God has given me an earthly temple to house my soul. It is my responsibility to take care of my body so I can do the other work God has called me to do. It is my responsibility to live a healthy lifestyle as a good example to my children.

You can read a full and current example of my Catholic Mom Manifesto on my website.

Get clear on what God has asked you to take care of. What are you a steward of? Next, you're going to create a vision for what you want to accomplish in each life facet: your mission.

Mission Statements

The first step in discovering your mission for each category is to think about the end of your life. How would someone describe your faith if they were giving the eulogy at your funeral? When someone asks your adult children what kind of mother you were, what do you want them to say? What kind of rest do you want to schedule into your life so you don't burn out chasing your dreams? What financial steps do you need to take to be financially secure in the future?

You want to imagine the best-version-of-yourself and write down what that looks like. Don't get caught up in getting this perfect, because it's likely this mission will change as time goes on. As you learn more about yourself, and as God gives you different blessings and different crosses, you'll adjust your mission. There will be times when you will pray and discern if your mission should change. It's important we are flexible about our mission statements so that we can allow God to sway us in directions that we hadn't considered before.

From a young age, I knew I wanted to be a public speaker. Every time I would attend a conference or a series of talks, I would watch the presenters with great awe and respect. Not only would I take notes on what they said, but also how they said things. I felt that this was going to be my future. When I was younger and didn't believe in God, I assumed I would end up talking about business or dog training.

If I had set this as my aim and been rigid about my dreams, I would never have opened my heart up to speaking about my Catholic faith. Now I look back and can see that God was preparing my heart all those years to be a Catholic evangelist.

We must surrender ourselves fully to Him, and in that surrender, we will discover His mission for our lives.

As we begin the process of praying and asking God what He wants us to do, recognize that life happens and plans change. It's important that we continue to go back to God and assess our mission for each facet of our life. When you ask God what He wants from you, don't try to force your dreams into His plan. Be open to what He has to say. Don't get too caught up in getting everything right when you make your plans. It's okay if they change, and it's likely they will.

I have often been inspired by this story of St. Louis de Montfort's faithfulness in the face of failure:

> *"In the town of Pontchâteau, St. Louis de Montfort inspired the peasants to build a huge monument to the Passion of Christ on a neighboring hill. For 15 months, hundreds of peasants volunteered their skills and labor to build it. When completed, it stood as a massive structure, a real labor of love, and on the day before it was supposed to be dedicated by the bishop, word got back to Louis that his enemies had convinced the government to destroy it. (They had lied to the authorities, saying that the structure was actually meant to be a fortress against the government.) When Louis received this disappointing news, he told the thousands of people who had gathered for the blessing ceremony, "We had hoped to build a Calvary here. Let us build it in our hearts. Blessed be God."[41]*

Sometimes God asks us to be faithful even when our plans crash and burn. I find great hope in this idea. It helps make me brave. It inspires me to try things I'm not sure I can accomplish, knowing that He can bring good out of anything, even failure.

Under each Stewardship Statement, you're going to write your Mission Statement. Your Mission Statement is what your long-term vision is for this area of your life: your aim. You're going to ask yourself what your mission is for each of the seven facets.

Mission Faith - Mission Motherhood
Mission Marriage - Mission Health
Mission Rest- Mission Finances
Mission Homemaking

Where do you want to be in twenty years? What kind of wife, mother, and Catholic do you want to be? What do you want people to say about you at your eulogy? We're talking hard questions, deep thoughts, and very long-term thinking here.

Pray and ponder those questions. Then you're going to write a few sentences about how you want your life to be in the future. You're going to write these in a present tense as if you have already accomplished your mission's aim.

Example Mission Health:

I am at a healthy weight for my life situation (pregnant, nursing, or not pregnant). I drink lots of water every day, and I nourish my body by eating mostly whole foods as my diet. I live an active lifestyle, and I work on strength training at least three days a week so I stay strong. I enjoy doing active things with my husband and my children. I turn off all my electronics at 7 p.m., and I get eight hours of sleep every night (if I don't have a baby.)

When I read that paragraph, I smile. It brings me peace to think of living a life like that. Of course, I may have to alter this in the future, but for now, I think it's a pretty accurate picture of how I would live a healthy lifestyle. It gives me something to shoot for.

Those are the aspects of health that are important to me. I don't have the parentheses in my own version because I know I will have different and reasonable weight/sleep plans if I'm pregnant or nursing. Take time to consider which aspects of your health are important to you.

My Mission Health is a summary of the healthy lifestyle I'm aiming for. Later we'll dive into smaller tasks like getting mammograms or taking vitamins, but we'll address those in our planning sessions. Right now we're trying to paint a big picture, a long-term vision.

Example Mission Marriage:

Our marriage is built on a foundation of Jesus and our great Catholic faith. I am a helpmate to my husband. I am constantly asking myself how I can help him to become a saint in Heaven. We have great communication, intimacy, and passion. We work hard and play hard together. We have a weekly date night and spend one weekend away together alone annually.

Your mission is something you're always working toward. Using my example, I will never be done working on communication or intimacy with my husband. I can always improve how I am my husband's helpmate. Because my husband and I feel so strongly that weekly date nights are part of the glue that holds our marriage together, this task makes it into my Mission Statement.

In Appendix A, I list a series of questions for each life facet to consider before writing your mission statement. Really sit with these questions before writing your mission statement. Write down honest answers.

We don't ask ourselves tough questions as often as we should. We don't challenge ourselves as much as we ought. The Catholic Mom Challenge is going to ask you the hard questions, and you should consider these before writing your Mission Statements.

Get Inspired

"Joy is very infectious; therefore, be always full of joy."
—St. Teresa of Calcutta[42]

For each of the seven life facets, I want you to pick a Bible verse or a quote that will help keep you inspired when the going gets tough. I have given you several examples for each of the seven facets in Appendix B. If you have a different verse you like, or a saint quote that really speaks to you, put that on your worksheet.

Sometimes I'm distracted by all the noise, pictures, and updates that surround me in daily life. They cloud my vision, and I forget what's important to me. That's when I lean on these quotes. A beautiful and simple quote can be an anchor in a world that's loud and ugly.

Later, you're going to be making your Catholic Mom Manifesto, which you can carry with you throughout the day. This guide will have all your inspirational quotes in it. It will be your anchor. You can color it. You can glue in pictures that are beautiful. This little booklet will help remind you of what you planted in faith - all the plans you made from a place of peace, love, and prayer.

For each life facet, you're going to have a Stewardship Statement, A Mission, and an Inspirational Quote.

Don't get too distracted by picking a quote now. We're going to set aside time for you to go through this exercise. Right now, I want you simply to read about all five steps of the Catholic Mom Challenge before diving in!

Assess Where You Are At

"You learn to speak by speaking, to study by studying, to run by running, to work by working, and just so, you learn to love by loving. All those who think to learn in any other way deceive themselves."
-St. Francis de Sales

This is the hardest step of the Catholic Mom Challenge for me – honestly assessing where I'm at in life. I have a difficult time being honest with myself, especially if I'm pouting like a teenager and I haven't spent much time with God lately. It's usually when I'm the busiest, most unhappy version of myself that I start dropping my prayer time and letting my daily Mass or Adoration habits slip.

You'd think I'd know better. You'd think I'd instantly lean on Jesus in times of trouble. Despite all I've learned and the deep faith I have, I still get distracted. I still believe the lies of the devil and of the world. I let my schedule take over and I allow it to keep me from spending time with Jesus.

The Catholic Mom Challenge helps us to create a built-in checkpoint each week to help you evaluate if you are getting distracted. You can spot these bad choices right away and then choose to get back on track quickly.

In this step, you're going to do an honest examination of your life as it currently is. You're going to write down what's working for you and what's not working.

Ladies, we can be really good at justifying our bad behavior. We can spin a good tale about why we had to do x or we couldn't really stop ourselves from doing y. We can make bad things sound good and make good things sound bad.

By lying when you work on this step, you will only hurt yourself.

This is the part of the challenge where you have to get real with yourself. This is between you and God. We have to get good at evaluating where we are with our lives. How did today go? How did the month go?

The good news is, I don't want you to feel bad if things have gone terribly wrong.

In fact, I don't want you to feel anything about the results at all. They are just that… results. I want us to look back at our day, our week, our month, or our year and simply write down what happened. What worked and what didn't work? Don't attach any emotions to it. We're just writing down data.

You are the scientist of your life, and you're just recording the results. Later in the book, I'll talk about what to do if being a perfectionist is holding you back. Right now I just want you to understand that, when you get to this step in the Catholic Mom Challenge, you need to be honest with yourself. Don't hold back. Tell it like it is.

Example of my Rest Assessment:

What's Working:

- Taking a bubble bath after the kids go to sleep relaxes me;
- I have positive, Catholic books to read on my kindle when I need to unwind;
- I feel rested after Michael takes the older girls on a four-plus hour adventure and I have quiet time to write and be with the baby.

What's Not Working:

- I'm not spending enough time in silence every day;
- I'm not managing my stress effectively – I let it overwhelm me too often;
- I still haven't figured out a restful activity we can do as a family on Sundays that everyone enjoys;
- I'm not turning off my phone every night at 7 p.m.

It's very difficult to make progress if you don't know what works for you and what doesn't work for you.

If your parents never taught you how to manage money, that is no longer an excuse. Own that you don't know how to manage money, and make a plan to learn how.

If you're not losing weight on this diet you're trying, ask yourself, did you really stick to it, or perhaps this particular diet is not right for you?

If your children are screaming all the time, ask yourself, what can you do to improve this situation? If you don't know the answer, ask some friends, read some parenting articles, or check out a book on discipline. Figure out if it's a phase that will pass or something you can change. Ask the women in the Catholic Mom Challenge Facebook group.

My hope is that, by creating a Catholic Mom Challenge community, we will form friendships and create a safe space where we can ask some of these questions. I'm hoping we will support each other with the lessons we've learned along the way and share helpful resources together.

The first time you fill out your Annual Planning worksheets, honestly assessing where you're at may be an emotional experience. It may be the first time you acknowledge the things that aren't working for you. Writing things down can sometimes feel like saying them out loud; this may be the first time you're owning these issues.

Don't let fear hold you back. You're going to be a great problem-solver this year, and you're going to become a much better version of yourself.

After you Assess Where You're At, you'll move on to Adjusting Your Aim.

Adjust Your Aim

"Freedom consists not in doing what we like, but in having the right to do what we ought."
-Saint John Paul II[43]

After you assess your situation, it's time to adjust your aim. Often times you won't need to make any adjustments to your annual plan unless something big has changed.

When my husband and I decided to move from Portland to Boise, we had to do a lot of adjusting to our plans. Even my holiday plans were suddenly going to be very different. I went through and adjusted my aim in many of the facets of my life.

Oftentimes, when I review my quarterly or monthly plans, I'll shuffle around which facet of my life is a top priority. There have been times when I feel that Michael and I aren't connecting, or worse, we're being snarky and short with each other. When I have assessed that my marriage is in a bad spot, I'll minimize the plans I had in the other facets of my life so that I can focus more on our marriage. This may involve planning a date night, reading a marriage book or finding a counselor to help us work through some issues.

This is the beauty of the program. You will honestly assess where things are, then shift your focus to where God is calling you. We'll talk more about discernment in the Actually Living It section of the book.

I make the most adjustments on my Weekly Planning worksheet. This is where I review what I have done for the week, including what worked and what didn't work. Then I plan what I'm going to tackle the next week.

For example, if I was hoping to drink sixty-four ounces of water every day, but didn't, then I try to figure out why. Did I not keep water with me? Was I being a baby about wanting cold or sparkling water? I acknowledge what went wrong, and then I adjust my aim.

I might lower my expectations for the next week. Maybe I'll start with forty-eight ounces of water and work my way up. Alternatively, I might focus on drinking 8 ounces of water before and after every meal. Maybe I'll fill up a large water bottle every time an alarm goes off on my phone. Maybe I'll slice up some lemons and keep flavored water in the fridge. These are all examples of how I've adjusted my aim based on my actual behavior.

After you have Adjusted Your Aim, you will move on to Make A Plan.

Make A Plan

"While the world changes, the cross stands firm."
— *St. Bruno*

The next step in the Catholic Mom Challenge system is to Make A Plan. You are going to list some specific tasks that will help you get closer to the long-term vision you have for your life. These tasks are likely what you used to call goals. Though we're not going to call them goals, we are still going to make sure they are S.M.A.R.T. That means they are specific, measurable, attainable, realistic, and time-bound.[44] These attributes are really important if you're serious about making progress.

If your hope for next year is to "get healthier." It's going to be hard to decide when or if you achieved this aim because it's not very specific. This example doesn't have a deadline and it's pretty vague.

Instead, it'd be much more powerful to say, "I will run for thirty minutes, three times per week." This is a very specific, measurable, and time-bound goal. Now, whether or not it's realistic or attainable is related to you and your present lifestyle.

Poorly written task: I will love my husband more.

Better task: I will schedule a weekly date night with my husband.

Poorly written task: I will pray more.

Better task: I will read my Magnificat and pray from 6-6:30 a.m. every morning.

You'll get better at creating tasks the more you set them and review them. We will go through the planning process annually, quarterly, monthly and weekly.

Annual Plan

"Great are those two gifts, wisdom and continence:
wisdom, forsooth, whereby we are formed in the
knowledge of God; continence whereby we are not
conformed to this world."
–St. Augustine

You will go through the Make a Plan process annually, quarterly, monthly and weekly. Your annual plan will take the most amount of time. You will want to create an annual plan no matter what month of the year you're picking up this book. Think of the natural rhythms of your life and pick the best month for you to do your Annual Planning. Many of you will choose January or August/September before school starts.

I like to do mine in January. In previous years, I would do my Annual Planning in September right before school starts. Pick a month that works for you. This first time, you may be making an Annual Plan for a partial year. Don't worry. Just start right now and then you'll start fresh when your chosen month arrives.

There is an Annual Planning document at www.catholicmomchallenge.com. Simply print it off and follow the steps!

Quarterly/Monthly Plan

The timing of your next planning session is up to you. I prefer to plan my life out three months at a time. I think of them as terms, an idea I got from Ashley Woleben, who blogs at www.betweenthelinens.com where she talks about homeschooling and living liturgically. I like planning my life three whole months at a time.

Because I personally enjoy the act of planning so much, planning itself can become a distraction for me. I can get sucked up in planning when I should be actually working. Therefore, it's good for me to schedule this only once a quarter. I make my Quarterly Plan by filling out three Monthly Planning pages. I write out what I'm doing for three months, and then try to stay on autopilot.

If your life changes a lot and you want to plan only a month ahead, do the Monthly Plan. I do not recommend doing the Quarterly Plan and the Monthly Plan, that's too much. Just pick which one you're going to do and stick with it. After you've done this, you'll break up your tasks into even smaller task that you'll assign in your Weekly Plan for the coming week.

Weekly Plan

Your weekly plan is going to look like a to-do list. It will include the things you want to tackle during the week. You'll make a plan each week and review it right before making next week's plan. You'll check in with yourself about what you accomplished. If you weren't able to complete some of the tasks on your to-do list, then you'll need to examine why.

In the next section, we'll talk about anticipating and overcoming obstacles. You'll be going through this process each time you make an Annual, Quarterly, Monthly or Weekly plan. It may sound like a lot when you're reading it all at once, but I promise, it's very simple. These activities are going to be very straightforward.

Anticipate and Prevent Obstacles

"Do not say that you have chaste minds if you have unchaste eyes, because an unchaste eye is the messenger of an unchaste heart."
—St. Augustine

This is a very important step that you will go through for each planning session you have. You don't want to skip this step. In this step, we need to lay our pride down. When we are prideful and full of ourselves, we're confident everything will go right. While it's good to have a positive attitude, it's naïve to assume all our plans will go smoothly.

For each planning session, we will list out the common pitfalls that might keep up from carrying out our mission or common obstacles that have held us back in the past. When you are doing this exercise, I want you to close your eyes and really imagine these obstacles coming up.

Let's say your goal is to cut out refined sugar and to lose 5 pounds. Then you're invited to a party. Rehearse what you're going to do when you're at this birthday party and you're offered a delicious cupcake. First, imagine yourself eating that cupcake in all its sugary glory. That will last approximately ninety seconds. Then imagine how badly you're going to feel having thwarted your health and weight loss plans. You're going to feel awful. The ninety seconds won't be worth it.

Now, imagine you say, "No thank you," with a smile. You're going to go home with a spring in your step! You're going to feel like a cupcake warrior! You're going to feel so proud of yourself when you step on the scale later.

I want you to really imagine the obstacles that are going to get in your way. Then I want you to come up with a plan for how you're going to overcome those obstacles when they pop up.

Here are some common obstacles that get in the way of my Mission Motherhood:

- I sleep in and don't wake up before the children;
- I don't drink enough or eat enough throughout the day, so I'm grumpy;
- I don't discipline the kids, so the kids walk all over me;
- I spend too much time on social media wishing for other people's things or situations.

Next, we come up with ways to prevent those obstacles or to overcome them when they appear.

- Go to bed at a reasonable time (after a digital sunset at 7 p.m.);
- Create a meal plan for the whole day and stick to it, including water!
- Communicate rules to the children and follow through with them, make a poster if you have to
- Limit time on social media, and when you feel jealous, stop and give thanks to God that He has blessed your friend.

You'll get better at this over time. The more you review what happened in your week, the more you will see patterns of obstacles that are getting in your way of pursuing your mission. You'll also get better at anticipating and squashing those obstacles.

For example, I have struggled with social media for many years. Recently, I've gotten better and I've limited how much time I spend on social media. When I see someone else's success, I give thanks to God for their good news instead of feeling bitter or jealous. I think this particular temptation affects many moms. We must learn how to protect ourselves emotionally to avoid succumbing to envy and jealousy when we log on.

My hope is that you can overcome some of your bad habits, too, even the ones you think have been ingrained for too long. Anything is possible with Christ. Because He is the center of our plan, we can draw on His strength to help us with our mission.

Chapter Ten:
Catholic Mom Manifesto

"My little children, reflect on these words: the Christian's treasure is not on earth but in heaven. Our thoughts, then, ought to be directed to where out treasure is. This is the glorious duty of man: to pray and to love."
–St. John Vianney

Now that we've covered the five steps, let's talk about what's going to be in your Catholic Mom Manifesto. You're going to love your Catholic Mom Manifesto! This is the moment my five-year-old would say, "Mom we don't love things, we love people." And she's right; words matter. So instead I'll say you're going to really treasure your Catholic Mom Manifesto.

This document, which is really going to end up being a little booklet you keep with you, is a summary of what's important to you. It will help keep you on track as you strive for sainthood. If you ever feel confused or distracted, you can pull this out, and it's like your very own life map.

I like the word manifesto because it feels like I'm declaring to the world that I want to be a saint!

I feel like I'm committing to something serious. And it is serious – the desire to be a saint! I want to love my husband, my kids, and my neighbors. I want to create a peaceful atmosphere in my home. I want to take care of my body and my finances. I want to rest and give thanks to the Lord for the life He's given to me.

If you don't like the word manifesto, you can easily pick Catholic Mom Map, Catholic Mom Manual, or something completely different. This little darlin' of a document is going to be your anchor. I'm going to give you some guidelines for things that absolutely have to be in there; you can be creative and add in personal touches as you like!

Don't worry about trying to remember everything right now. You're going to find worksheets and a step-by-step guide for filling them out on my website. This is just meant to give you an idea of what the process is going to look like. Later, you'll schedule a big chunk of time to go through these steps.

Components of your Catholic Mom Manifesto

Each facet of your life is going to have your Stewardship Statement, Mission Statement, and an Inspirational Quote. These are things that are not likely to change for the entire year. Again, if big life changes happen, you may want to go through and update a section of your book. Alternatively, you may choose to leave them as they are and update these sections when you do your Annual Planning. My Catholic Mom Manifesto doesn't change very often.

Here are some of the worksheets we will fill out:

- Tips for Success that are specific to you;
- Common Obstacles and ways to overcome them;
- A STOP Doing List of activities that keep you from being your best;
- Signs You're Out of Tune with God so you can recognize them more clearly when they appear.

These sections are more personal, so some of you may not want to put them in your booklet. I personally would rather risk someone seeing the details of what I struggle with than to not have my plan with me at all.

I highly recommend reading the last section of this book, *Actually Living It*, before you make your Catholic Mom Manifesto. I mention a lot of strategies for setting yourself up for success and avoiding common pitfalls. Having this information before you make your plan can really help you design a more realistic, and ultimately, a more successful plan.

Chapter Eleven:
Putting It All Together

You're going to schedule time to design and create your Catholic Mom Manifesto. It will probably take about two to three hours. You'll want to be uninterrupted and in a place that makes you feel calm and peaceful.

Don't worry, you don't need to be artistic to do this. I certainly don't have an artistic bone in my body. When I try adult coloring, it looks like my five-year-old did it. The value of this booklet is the information inside, not how pretty the outside is.

I like to start in an Adoration chapel and then finish at a coffee shop I like. I've also had years where I do this in twenty-minute bursts in my jammies in my bedroom, so do what works for you!

Here is the Catholic Mom Manifesto process:

- Write your Stewardship Statement and Mission Statement for each life facet;
- Choose an inspirational quote for each life facet;
- Fill out Life Planning worksheet assessing where you're at and making plans for going forward;
- Get more specific when you make your Annual, Quarterly Monthly, and Weekly plan;
- Fill out your Keys To Success worksheet;
- Identify obstacles and ways to overcome those obstacles;
- Write down your STOP Doing List;
- Write down the ways you'll know you're Out of Tune with God;
- Create your Catholic Mom Manifesto booklet;
- **Then start living the Catholic Mom Challenge!**

To see a full example, you can look at a current copy of my Catholic Mom Manifesto on my website. I have added in extra things to mine, like the mysteries of the Rosary and my Marian consecration prayer. If you'd like to follow me through this process, I have videos on my website taking you through each section.

After you go through this process, you might be feeling really excited to start living your life in the Catholic Mom Challenge way. If you're like me, however, you might be terrified that even though you made an outstanding plan, you're worried you're going to screw it up.

The last part of this book is about how you're actually going to use this system day in and day out. These are the tips and tricks for being a successful Catholic mom in today's modern world. Again, I recommend reading these steps *before* you create your Catholic Mom Manifesto because many of the tips might surprise you!

Part Three:

What To Do When *Life* Happens

What To Do When *Life* Happens

"If you are what you should be, you will set the whole world ablaze!"
– St. Catherine of Sienna

This is my favorite part of the book! Here I will explain the little ways you can set yourself up for success, avoid self-sabotage, and turn into an efficient, good-habits-driven, super rockin' Catholic mom!

I want you to turn to these pages often when you need a little tough love or an attitude boost. I'm hoping this section of the book is going to feel like a phone call from your best friend who helps you get out of your funk.

These are the tips I've gathered from all my favorites: Matthew Kelly, Brian Johnson, Fr. John Riccardo, Ashley Woleban, Crystal Paine, Michael Hyatt, and all the other self-help, business books, and blogs I've read over the years.

I discovered many of the ideas in this section by watching Optimal Living 101 videos from Brian Johnson. He reads dozens of books each year and then creates a summary of them. Membership to his website costs $10/month to access all these videos. I'm pretty frugal but I consider this the best money I spend each month! I watch these videos for motivation, new ideas, and help to stay focused on my dream of being a saint.

Read on and soak up this wisdom. Apply it to your life. Imprint it into your brain. These are the keys to living a successful, peaceful life as you strive for sainthood.

Chapter Twelve:
Set Yourself Up For Success

If you're reading this book, chances are you've gone through some sort of self-help program before. You want to be a better Catholic, a more romantic wife, a calmer mother, or a healthier version of yourself. It's important to set yourself up for success in the Catholic Mom Challenge.

We're going to start by making sure you believe in yourself. If you're anything like me and you've tried several diet plans, many different types of planners, a few schooling techniques and even counseling, maybe you're doubting whether this program can really help you.

This next section is all about picking yourself up, dusting off those negative thoughts, and feeling confident as you make your new plan for your life.

I know you can find peace in your life. I also know that God has a plan for you to fulfill the desires of your heart because He placed them there. Achieving sainthood will absolutely take you outside of your comfort zone, but it is the ultimate satisfaction we can ever experience.

Once you get clear that striving for sainthood is your purpose in life, you can get clarity on your priorities and find peace in how you live your life. By fully understanding your motivation for everything you take on, you can find joy even in the mundane tasks you have to accomplish.

Believe You CAN

"In Him you also, when you had heard the word of truth,
the gospel of your salvation, and had believed in Him,
were marked with the seal of the promised Holy Spirit."
— St. Paul

I was thinking about the word "self-esteem" the other day. I was imagining my daughters in their teen years. What could I do to give them a strong foundation of faith and life experiences, so they have good self-esteem by the time they hit those awkward teen years? While I was thinking about that, I also had to ask myself, "Do I have good self-esteem?"

It's a silly question because we often reserve discussion about self-esteem for teens and single people. It's as if, once we get married, no one brings up self-esteem anymore. We tend to switch gears and talk about whether or not we think we are good mothers, good wives, or good Catholics. Those aspects of ourselves are different than reflecting on our own self-esteem.

You need to believe in yourself.

You need to feel confident in yourself.

We should all have good self-esteem because the Lord of the universe, who created every beautiful thing on our planet, chose to create us and place us in this location at this time. If that doesn't make you feel loved and special, then I think you need to work on getting to know the God of the universe better.

One of my major life goals is to be an opening speaker for Matthew Kelly at a Catholic conference. I greatly admire Matthew Kelly, and it would be such an honor to speak at the same event as him. If this happened, if MK's people called me and invited me to speak at an event, I would freak out. This would be like going to the Grammys for me! I would lose my mind with excitement and jump around my room like an excited eleven-year-old girl. I can imagine bursting with excitement!

Now imagine your own special moment. Who would you love to meet? Who would you love as a running mate in a marathon? Who would you love to autograph a book for you? This isn't about famous people; it's about people we are in awe of.

Think of that person you greatly admire. Now realize, they're just a common human being.

They will eventually die. It's likely they won't be remembered in a hundred years. This person is just a blink of an eye compared to our God who created all things. I'm not putting down a person of whom you are in great awe, but shouldn't our amazement be one thousand times greater for our Lord? Shouldn't we be incredibly humbled and flattered that He chose to create us?

This concept is hard for us to process. My body gets physically excited, my pulse quickens; and I feel butterflies in my stomach just *thinking* about standing on stage with Matthew Kelly. But my body doesn't feel like that when I think about Jesus. Even though it is my entire life's goal to stand in front of Jesus and to have Him be pleased with me; it feels so far away. My brain can't even conjure up that situation because it's so beyond me.

That is precisely why we must be faithful, though. Our feelings can lie and our flesh is sinful. Yet, God gave us both our intellect and the Church to keep us from falling into self-indulgence and instead, to truly come to love and serve Him. Love is not a feeling. It is not about feelings. Loving the Lord may never make my heart race, but this is what I am called to do.

This is what you're called to do too. You are incredibly special. God loves you so much. You should have a tremendous amount of self-esteem because of this.

Breaking Trust With Ourselves

Our self-esteem can also be damaged when we break trust with ourselves. Many adults lack self-esteem because they are constantly breaking promises they make to themselves. This is one of the ways I saw my self-confidence start to crumble after becoming a mom. I would set out to do things and then when I'd fail, I'd feel awful.

"Okay, this week I'm going to actually do the chores on my chart and keep this house clean."

"Reading is important, so I'm going to spend at least thirty minutes per day reading books to my daughter."

"I will make dinner every single night this week and have it ready when my husband gets home."

"I am going to lose my baby weight within six months of having my daughter."

It doesn't matter what these promises were, and it really doesn't matter what was keeping me from completing them. A big consequence of not completing these tasks was that I was losing trust in myself. I no longer believed that what I said I was going to do, was actually going to get done.

When you don't trust yourself, you feel yucky inside. Sometimes you even begin to feel dead inside.

The more you break trust with yourself, the more you are going to experience low self-esteem. As married women with children, it can be confusing to have low self-esteem. You're already married, you already have kids, and maybe you own a beautiful home. In a sense, all those things you were dreaming about are here. But if you don't trust yourself, or if you have low self-esteem, the dream can feel like it's covered in slime.

The good news is that *you* are the cause of your own low self-esteem. It's actually pretty easy to turn this around once you recognize that you simply need to trust yourself again.

When I'm feeling down and I think nothing is working, the first question I ask myself is, "Have I broken trust with myself?" I recall recent promises I've made to myself or to others that I haven't been able to keep. Most of the time, I've let myself down because I had unrealistic goals and expectations. When I didn't accomplish what I wanted to, I felt guilty and disappointed.

How I Build My Self-Esteem Back Up

1. Identify the promises I broke;
2. Figure out if I should keep them or not (Were they unreasonable or were they completely attainable? Was I just being lazy?);
3. Cross off the ones that are unreasonable;
4. Schedule time to complete the ones I still want to complete;
5. Add in a few small promises to get the ball rolling.

That's the process I go through, usually after I've had a good cry. Perhaps I thought that the world was ending, I'd never leave Toddlerland, or my marriage would never work. After my pity party, I take a deep breath. I step back and realize I've probably broken trust with myself and that I need to turn it around. My bad attitude is because of my low self-confidence, and I need to get my Mama Mojo back!

Step number five is the most important. I have to pick a few small things I want to do and *do* them right away so I can start creating a momentum of wins in my life. The more of these little wins I have, the cheerier I feel.

I might start by cleaning my kitchen sink so it sparkles! I might spend ten minutes reading books to the girls. There's something about the purity of reading books to my kids that snaps me out of a bad mood. I might do fifteen squats and fifteen push-ups right away. I might surprise my husband with a genuine kiss for no reason.

These are small things, but if I can knock them out, they will start to make me feel better about myself. My self-esteem goes up, and I feel stronger and more able to tackle some of the bigger things. I try to make these activities seem fun. I even try to make a game out of them.

Can I clean all the bathrooms in the house in thirty minutes? Can I wash and fold every single piece of laundry in the house? *Let's do this!* I'm going to sort every piece of mail and pay all the bills before my girls wake up, so where are those stamps?

I want to take a moment to say that if you're suffering from clinical depression, these five steps aren't likely to get you out of your funk. Sometimes we really just need counseling or medication to help us. If you're not sure whether you have clinical depression or not, visit your doctor to discuss what you're going through.

Get Out Of Your Comfort Zone

"If a man wishes to be sure of the road he treads on, he
must close his eyes and walk in the dark."
– St. John of the Cross

If you're going to achieve any self-growth at all, you'll need to get out of your comfort zone. As Americans, we're trained to seek comfort and pleasure. We like places and activities that are familiar to us. This practice of staying in familiar and common situations often prevents us from growing.

I'm not talking about leaving the comfort of maintaining traditions in your household. Celebrating Catholic rhythms that are the same every year is a wonderful way to bring liturgy into your home. Instead, I'm talking about the comfort we choose when we stay at home in our pajamas instead of going to a Bible study. Perhaps we don't want to expend the energy it takes to meet new people or to be vulnerable in a group.

One of the biggest ways you can set yourself up for success in the Catholic Mom Challenge is to prepare yourself to step outside of your comfort zone.

"This is going to be difficult, but it's going to be valuable."

"I will be a better person for having gone through this."

Whether you are shaking up your relationships, instilling new habits, or diving more deeply into your Catholic faith, the unknown can be scary. Instead of allowing fear to creep into your heart, though, just acknowledge that it is, in fact, unknown. The task may be new and difficult, but you are fighting for eternity here. You are striving for sainthood, and that will mean painful growth.

Close your eyes again and picture Jesus laying His hand on your shoulder and saying, "Well done, good and faithful servant." Matthew 25:21 Isn't this praise more important than your fears?

I am constantly having to give myself a pep talk. I don't like going outside of my comfort zone. Although attending Catholic conferences is one of my favorite activities, I often wake up that morning thinking to myself, "I'd rather stay in bed and do nothing today."

I know that conferences are often emotionally draining. It's likely I will be challenged by what the speakers say and I will be exhausted by the end of the day. Yet, I always feel so alive after a conference and am glad, when the day is over, that I went. Most conferences are filled with great gems of wisdom that I can apply to my life!

I have to ignore the lies of the devil to pursue things that are good, even if they are outside my comfort zone.

I know that my feelings lie and that my resting state of laziness and shyness keeps me from being the woman that God has called me to be. I'm sure there are little demons who sit on my shoulder and whisper, "It's going to be so uncomfortable to meet new people. You'll have to share really personal things with them. You know you get tired after four hours of chatting."

If you don't believe in demons, read *The Screwtape Letters* by C.S. Lewis.[45]

As I've grown spiritually, I've gotten better at spotting these lies in my thoughts. I'm better at being a cheerleader for myself and keeping my eyes fixed on Jesus. I know what I need to do to become a better version of myself, and I don't let the negative voices in my head trick me into choosing a worse path.

When I'm feeling particularly insecure or fearful, I just tell myself, "Sterling, it's time to put your big girl pants on and get this done." I try to move forward as quickly as possible without dwelling on my fear. If you struggle with fear, I would recommend reading *The Other Side of Fear* by Hallie Lord.[46] It's a lovely book that will help you feel brave.

Be bold. Commit to living outside your comfort zone. If you need to give yourself fifty pep talks today, do it. The buck stops with you. You are the only one who is going to be accountable for whether or not you go to Heaven for eternity.

The Motivation Equation

*"We always find that those who walked closest to Christ
were those who had to bear the greatest trials."*
– St. Teresa of Avila

I have big dreams; I always have. One of my gifts from God has always been vision. I can see what's possible whether it's for a business, in my home, for my children, or for a book I want to write. I can easily picture what I want or where something needs to go. That doesn't mean I'm good at achieving these things, though. Sometimes I lack the motivation to take a shower.

Ridiculous, right? I can dream up a ten-year business plan, but the idea of taking off my clothes, getting my hair wet, being cold, and having to pick out new clothes sounds exhausting to me.

Whether you're tackling big dreams or little tasks, your success will come down to your motivation. How motivated are you to get this done? There's no fooling yourself about motivation. You either have enough of it to get your task done, or you don't.

Previously we discussed the danger posed by traditional goal setting. From now on, when I use the word goals, I want you to remember that a good goal needs to be translated into discrete habits and tasks.

I can tell myself all day long that teaching Latin to my daughter is important. If the program is collecting dust on my shelf and I put it off every day, though, the truth is I'm not motivated enough to get it done.

Before you beat yourself up over not being motivated enough, let's take a look at the Motivation Equation[47] to see if we can figure out what's going wrong. This is something I got from Brian Johnson who studied the work of Piers Steel,[48] a leading psychologist in procrastination and motivation. Here's the motivation equation:

$$Motivation = \frac{Expectancy \; x \; Value}{Impulsiveness \; x \; Delay}$$

Let's start by breaking down what's in the numerator: how much you believe you can achieve this goal multiplied by how much you value this goal. I like to look at value first.

Value: Is the thing I'm trying to accomplish really important to me? Some things are easy to assess, like my desire to be a saint in Heaven. Yes, I absolutely want to accomplish this in my lifetime!

Some things are more difficult to sort out, like wanting to teach my daughter Latin. When push comes to shove, how important is this to me? Do I think she can be happy without learning this? Do I think we really need to spend the extra time doing this? Is it going to make our family stronger?

After assessing how much I value my goal, I either scratch it off my list, because I realize it's just not that important to me, or I keep it on my list and take a look at expectancy.

Expectancy: Do I really believe it's possible to achieve this goal? This can be a hard one to really ask yourself. Often times I have to admit that, no, I really don't think I can achieve this goal. I don't believe I can lose thirty pounds and keep it off. I don't think I'll ever have a fantastic sex life. I don't believe I'll ever be able to carve out time for self-care and rest.

When you don't actually believe your goal is possible, you have to do one of two things: either get rid of the goal entirely, or break your goal into more manageable, and therefore believable, parts.

Some goals are simply unreasonable for you in your current reality; you should let these goals go. Because I am optimistic by nature, I frequently get excited and believe I really can do everything. Maybe I volunteered for too many activities and then find myself unable to keep up with the basic needs of my family. In this situation, it is responsible for me to back out of some commitments.

Alternatively, you may have a goal that is simply too ambitious. In this case, you should adjust your goal to be more reasonable. For example, losing five pounds a week was never really going to happen. You can instead target one pound per week. Don't be afraid to make your goal "stupid easy"[49] to help you build some initial momentum.

If you're struggling to get an hour of prayer done every day, perhaps you could commit to praying for five minutes per day instead. After succeeding at this level, you can slowly aim for more.

Don't feel discouraged! Remember, we are working towards building up personal trust and your self-esteem so you can have more peace and feel more contentment in your life. This is a process. God does not want you to live your life immersed in anxiety, guilt, frustration, or anger. The key to avoiding these things is to really understand and master yourself. Start by examining your motivation, or lack thereof.

Next, we'll look at the bottom of the Motivation Equation: Impulsiveness x Delay.

Impulsiveness: How distracted are you while trying to reach your goal? When I was a new mom, I cleaned the house only when I felt like it, which was practically never. It was easy to let things distract me from getting taking care of my home.

"Oh! I need to pay the bills."

"I really should take Rose for a walk to the park today."

"What am I going to make for dinner? Maybe I'll plan something new!"

None of those things are bad, but they are all distractions. I'm allowing my impulses to get the better of me; I flit from one thing to the next, letting important tasks go undone. After two weeks of a messy house not getting cleaned, it's time for me to evaluate what's failing in the Motivation Equation.

If something is really important to me, and I believe I can achieve it (the top half of the Motivation Equation), I take a look at what impulsive behavior is getting in the way.

In the example of the bathroom, I needed to create a block of time each day to focus on house chores and to treat it like an actual commitment. Right now we do our chores after 10 a.m. snack; the children all have come to expect this. I've put it on my daily schedule and communicated it to my family. This was my solution to contain my impulsiveness so I could get my chores done.

I also discovered that my phone was one of the reasons I wasn't getting as much done during the day as I wanted. I let my phone interrupt me all day long. Whether it was pinging from a notification or I was compulsively checking for updates, it would distract me from my important work.

Now, I have two docking stations (one upstairs and one downstairs) where I keep my phone. I turned off all push notifications, except actual phone calls, and I only check it at certain times throughout the day. Those times are actually planned out. This might sound ridiculous, but how much more could you do if you didn't touch your phone for several two-hour blocks each day?

You have to ask yourself who you want to be and what you want to get done. Are you setting yourself up for success?

Finally, we will examine the last component of the Motivation Equation.

Delay: This is how long it will take you to reach your goal. If your goal is twenty years away, it's tough to keep your motivation up each day. The best solution is to decrease the delay by breaking up your goal into smaller goals with intermediate dates. This will increase your motivation.

If you need to lose fifty pounds, start by focusing on the first five. Pick a small reward to give yourself when you accomplish this. If you want to be debt free, start with your smallest debt. Make a goofy thermometer that you fill in as you pay down your debt. You can hit that goal much faster than paying off everything you owe. If even that is too big, then just work toward paying off $100 at a time!

The smaller your goal, the faster you'll reach it. This will build up your personal trust and provide you additional motivation to keep moving forward and achieve more of your goals! Goals should always be measurable, so you should be able to cut them down into smaller bites. If they're not measurable, that's the first problem you need to solve. You need to work on being able to track your progress in some quantifiable way.

Understanding the Motivation Equation can help you examine your lack of progress. If you're lacking the motivation to get something done, check in with these four parameters and see which one needs tweaking. I'm constantly reviewing my to-do list and asking myself, "Why don't I feel motivated to get this done?" Usually, I just need an attitude check and to remind myself that it is really valuable to me and that I do expect to achieve it. Sometimes I do have to make an adjustment.

When something is important to you, you'll move mountains to get it done! Trust me, with Jesus on your side, you can do anything!

Chapter Thirteen:
Willpower and Good Habits

When it comes down to it, most of us struggle with a shortage of willpower. We think we struggle with discipline, but really it's willpower that we lack. I'm going to break down the difference between discipline and willpower so you can use these two resources to build a life around good habits.

We want to train ourselves to identify and get rid of our bad habits and to instill healthy and productive habits instead. This can be difficult if you don't understand the basic principles of why some habits stick and some habits don't.

We're going to start by keeping the bar low so you can build some momentum of success. I want you to genuinely believe that you can make progress in an area of your life that you've always struggled with. By the grace of God and with the help of Jesus, you can do anything.

Take a deep breath and be committed to discarding all your negative thoughts about how you've failed before. This is a turning point.

Willpower

"The nation doesn't simply need what we have. It needs what we are."
— St. Teresa Benedicta (Edith Stein)[50]

In this section, I want to draw a distinction between three things: feelings, discipline, and willpower. I believe these often get jumbled together but should be treated very differently. People mistake one for another, making it hard to find success. Because the solution to overcoming each is different, it's hard to progress if you mistake which one you're dealing with. My goal is to help you understand all three.

Feelings

First, let's address feelings – I believe it's the most frequently misunderstood. Our society tells us that we should do "whatever we feel like doing."

"Do whatever feels good."

"Give in to your feelings."

"How does that make you feel?"

"I'm just crazy and emotional when I'm pregnant."

"I can't help it."

Because God made women to be nurturing and receptive beings, we have very strong feelings. It's easy for us to let them take over and guide our actions. While feelings are good and can be a strong indication of what is going on in our lives, they should not dictate how we act.

Sometimes, my husband may do something incredibly annoying, and I feel irritated and frustrated with him. I could grab my keys, leave the house, and get a separate apartment so I could live alone. Most people would say this is an overreaction.

I want to challenge us, however, because many of us overreact on a much smaller scale, letting our emotions rule us, while still feeling that our behavior is justified.

When my children create a mess, I feel frustrated. I might react to this feeling by speaking to them in a rude, disrespectful, and angry tone. Now, what they did could be wrong, and I could very well *feel* frustrated, but it does not justify being rude and disrespectful to my kids. I should instead have control over myself so I can calmly explain the problem, discipline as needed, and move on.

I think women have bought the lie that we're emotional and we simply can't control ourselves. We believe that it's okay for women to "freak out" or "to be super pissed" or "to be an angry mommy." We even joke about this!

We lose our tempers with our husbands and somehow feel as if we have a feminine right to do this. Worse, in the same breath, we may be telling our husbands they have to work on their own anger problems.

Nothing has the power to "make us angry".[51] Giving in to anger is always a choice, and it's almost always the wrong choice. Don't get me wrong, I'm not talking about righteous anger, which is okay (but rare.) Righteous anger would be a just response to the fact that unborn babies are being killed by the millions. Although, it's okay to be angry about that, you still have to act in a just proportion.

There are a few situations that call for righteous anger. Most often, when we are speaking out of anger, we are doing so in a sinful way. I want to focus on our tendency to excuse ourselves for our sinful reactions to anger.

Feelings of pain and frustration are not wrong. Imagine that your husband comes home and tells you he spent $1,500 on a new TV without first discussing the purchase with you. It's perfectly okay for you to feel hurt and disrespected by his decision. I would also feel minimized. You might be tempted to indulge these feelings and respond in anger. Screaming at him in a disrespectful way, or leaving your marriage over this, are not appropriate responses.

Recognize the reaction that's taking place in your mind and attempt to calm down. If you're unable to have a calm discussion with your husband, you need to wait until you can. When you are able, sit down with your husband and calmly explain that what he did caused you to feel hurt.

We don't have control over what God puts in our path. Life will always be unpredictable. The only thing we really have control over is how we react. This boils down to willpower. I need to separate my feelings from my reaction and use my willpower to respond in a Christian way.

It is important to understand that our feelings bubble up all the time. A feeling is something completely externally caused. For example, if I pinch your arm, you have no choice but to feel the pain. You do have a choice, however, about responding in anger. What if I am a doctor preparing to administer a shot? Now, instead of feeling angry, you might feel thankful.

Here is a more difficult example. Imagine your mother-in-law criticizes your parenting style in front of your children. Clearly, in this case, an injustice has occurred. You have very little choice about feeling hurt. It's an emotional wound much like a physical wound. When people hurt us emotionally like this, we begin to feel unsafe around them.

Our response may be to put our guard up and respond in anger. Instead, I encourage you to consider the example of our Lord. When He was hurt, He responded with meekness and humility. Very few of us are yet mature enough to consistently choose this response, myself included. While the injustice may be very real, our goal should be no less than to imitate our Lord. When we fall short of this and react in anger, we must apologize when we are calm.

It's important that you control your reaction to your mother-in-law. Don't ignore her or let your temper boil after she leaves, never dealing with the issue head on. You should calm down, then have a rational discussion with her. If you don't have a close relationship with her, you might task your husband with discussing this issue with her. If you blew it and yelled at her, you should apologize for your outburst no matter how hard this is. An apology doesn't justify her behavior but you will have taken responsibility for yours.

I personally struggle with controlling my responses in my marriage. I sometimes feel that the marriage relationship gives me permission to be my worst. I would never speak to my friends in the awful way I sometimes speak to my husband. There is no excuse for this. While I may feel justified about my position on the topic we are discussing, it is never appropriate for me to raise my voice, throw sarcastic barbs at him, or use crying in a manipulative way. Sometimes it takes all the strength I can muster to apologize for my behavior, especially if I still think he was wrong. I must do it anyways.

God wants us to have peace. He wants us to be content. We must work hard to acknowledge our feelings as feelings, then act in a responsible and calm way.

Another time when I struggle with self-control is when I am pregnant. When I'm pregnant I feel I can eat all the food, take all the naps, and be a crazy person to everyone in my family. Sure, food, naps, and hormones are all an important part of pregnancy. Too often, however, we take advantage of pregnancy stereotypes and use them as an excuse for gluttony, laziness, and rude behavior.

Let's move on to discipline.

Discipline

Discipline is a trained behavior that we don't have to focus on. For example, you have to put your shoes on before you go outside. You don't think about this. You don't wonder if maybe today you should leave the house without shoes. You just do it; it's automatic.

There is no willpower involved when we put on our shoes. It's routine. It's a habit. Discipline is easier to apply to familiar routines. Discipline is the result of cultivating good habits. Over time, these habits become automatic and don't require either intentional willpower or emotional energy.

You just wake up at 6 a.m. every morning, that's what you do.

You do the laundry on Mondays, that's what you do.

You pray the Divine Mercy Chaplet in the 3 p.m. hour, that's what you do.

We use willpower to create discipline through habits. It requires an incredible amount of willpower initially, but once routines and habits (discipline) are established, the willpower required to carry them out feels comparatively small. Understanding this is key to becoming the best-version-of-yourself. Most successful people have mastered the process of cultivating new habits to create discipline and liberate willpower for other challenges.

Willpower

Willpower is different from both feelings and discipline. Unlike feelings, we do have a choice with what we do with our willpower. We can choose to push through our feelings. Willpower is used to make emotionally difficult decisions. Unlike discipline, willpower is both a conscious act and a finite resource. Many people often complain, "I cannot do this because I lack discipline." Instead, it's likely they are unwilling to spend the willpower to create the discipline. This may be a conscious or subconscious decision.

Willpower is finite, like a battery. It runs out. If you have to make 50 decisions before 9 a.m., you may not have enough willpower to make good choices for the rest of the day. This is often called decision fatigue   you have simply depleted your willpower. As more of your daily decisions become automatic, you retain more willpower later in the day.

For example, I struggle to drink enough water during the winter. I never feel like drinking cold water so I keep putting it off. To overcome this, I cultivated the habit of brewing 8 cups of tea in the morning. Now, I don't have to fight with myself throughout the day to get enough water. I genuinely enjoy the tea, and because I make it automatically every morning, I no longer spend willpower on this task. It has become a discipline for me that is no longer emotional.

Understanding and cultivating willpower is essential to your success. Willpower out predicts I.Q. for academic performance by a factor of two.[52] This is big news! If you've ever felt as if you're not very smart, understand that you could be more successful than someone with a higher I.Q. if you learn how to manage your willpower.

As you implement the Catholic Mom Challenge, I want you to notice how you spend your willpower throughout the day.

Willpower, like all virtues, improves with practice. You can cultivate a deeper and stronger will in yourself, by overcoming short-term desires and feelings in favor of long-term rewards. While this process can be painful, it's worth it.

Learning to cultivate my own willpower has helped me tremendously. Previously, I allowed feelings of anger, frustration, fear and anxiety to rule my actions. As my discipline improves and I have more willpower available, I am able to spend it to regain self-control.

I used to get upset with my children and yell at them out of anger and frustration. After reading Head and Heart[53], I decided that I wanted to cultivate more peace in my home. I often say to myself as I'm preparing to interact with my family, "I am the peace center of my home." This habit has helped me to keep my temper down and to remember that I always get to choose how I react. I still give my children timeouts, but I do so in a calm and firm voice.

I have more emotional energy throughout the day to tackle other challenges because I do not waste that energy on anger.

We need to teach ourselves and our children about willpower.

It's crucial that we not only work on our own willpower, but we train our children to understand their own willpower as well. We must teach our children to control their impulses, to instill healthy habits so they don't experience decision fatigue by mid-afternoon, and to teach them about willpower. If we do this, their chances of success are far greater than if we simply have naturally smart kids.

Finally, you need to learn to recognize when you're not properly managing your willpower. If you consistently feel overwhelmed and are choosing the short-term pleasures, then it's time to shift your willpower budget around. One tip is to try and tackle the things you struggle with in the morning.

For example, if you struggle to cook dinner and frequently want to order pizza, try to prepare dinner in the morning when your willpower is strong. Then all you have to do is heat it up in the evening when your willpower is low. Pre-load as many hard tasks as you can in the beginning of the day.

I hope that a better understanding of how willpower works will help you to efficiently create habits and streamline your life.

Bad Habits Out, Good Habits In

Humans can accomplish amazing things. When I think about the incredible discipline and willpower of some of the people I admire, it makes me want to work harder and stretch myself. The more I study the lives of successful people, the more I see patterns of good habits. They wake up early, journal, eat healthy food, exercise, minimize distractions, focus on what's important to them, and, for many who are religious, they pray and go to Mass.

One of the keys to finding peace and meaning in life, or becoming the best-version-of-yourself, is to use your willpower to instill new habits. You want to use your fresh willpower in the morning to create a new system and instill it as a habit. After thirty to ninety days, when the habit becomes ingrained, you won't need to think about it anymore. That system is now on autopilot, and you can use your willpower to create another one.

We want to avoid decision fatigue. How many decisions do you have to make before 11 a.m.? I bet it's a lot, maybe even a hundred! The more routines you can put on autopilot, the more willpower you will retain throughout the day. Then you'll have more energy to devote to things that really matter.

Sometimes I have to create a Stop-Thinking-About list so I stop wasting energy chewing on the problems that aren't really important or timely. It often includes:

- Your house is fine; you don't need to move;
- You're going to homeschool the kids this year; stop looking at schools and other curricula;
- You don't need to review your budget; staring at the excel boxes isn't going to change anything;
- Yes, you want to visit your family in Michigan, but it's not a possibility now; reevaluate this in three months instead of dwelling on it daily.

What issues do you turn over in your mind constantly that never seem to have a resolution? Write them down so your brain can pop up a red flag when you start wasting emotional energy on issues you can't solve right now.

In addition to creating new, healthy habits, also think about the bad habits you need to *stop* doing. We all have bad habits and addictions holding us back. Spend some time thinking about the bad habits that you need to stop doing. If you can, replace each bad habit with a positive habit.

Here are some habits I have stopped in the past or would still like to stop:

- Reading fiction that's not outstanding (e.g. bad, young adult fiction or romance novels);
- Eating fast food, ever;
- Drinking too much alcohol (I can enjoy one glass of alcohol without it affecting my sleep or giving me a headache);
- Watching inappropriate television (this has largely been made possible through just plain not watching things with bad content or editing out bad content using VidAngel[54].);
- Picking at my lips when they're dry.

I recommend only working on one habit at a time. It's okay to replace a bad habit with a new, good habit because that's still only cultivating one new habit. Don't tackle more than one at a time, focus your willpower.

Getting Habits To Stick

"You cannot be half a saint; you must be a whole saint or no saint at all."
– St. Therese of Lisieux

Once you have created a list of habits and have picked the very first one you're going to work on, go all in. Make one hundred percent commitment to yourself and set clear boundaries. Lawyers have this term called *bright lines*.[55] They say a good contract has bright lines that are so obvious, you would never cross them. You want your habit to have bright lines.

For example, if you say, "I'm going to drink less alcohol," you'll constantly be wondering, "Is this special occasion special enough? Well, I am at a party with my friends, so that's probably okay, right? I've had such a hard day today; just one glass of wine."

You'll start bargaining with yourself. It's harder to maintain a "sometimes" good habit than it is to commit one hundred percent. If you simply said, "Alcohol is bad for me. I don't need it in my life, and it's holding me back from becoming the best-version-of-myself. I won't drink ever again." Then it would be easier to never drink alcohol again than to constantly be wondering if tonight was one of the exceptions.

I suggest you create a bright line about your prayer life. Make it a non-negotiable habit. You're going to pray in the morning right after you wake up. Even if your kids are crying and you slept in, you pray a Hail Mary and thank God for the day before getting out of bed. Though this solution isn't ideal, at least the first words out of your mouth are to praise the Lord. There are no "days off" of prayer. There are no exceptions.

Commit to starting a new habit or working on kicking out a bad one. Don't start by tackling twenty habits. Just pick one, remove negotiation, and just *do it*.

Whatever you decide to work on, do it daily. You don't want to exercise Monday, Wednesday, and Friday. Every time you take a day off, you lose momentum. You don't need to do a hardcore workout every day. Maybe you do light stretching or go for a walk on Tuesday and Thursday. If this lifestyle change is important to you and is helping you to strive for sainthood, do something every day.

It's hard to maintain any habit that's not daily. If you skip a day when you're on a M/W/F schedule, now you've gone three days without working on your habit. Suddenly, you'll find you've dropped it altogether. The amount of willpower it takes to push through your guilt and sense of failure to start again is tremendous. Don't set yourself up to fail. Start all your habits as daily habits.

This may sound overwhelming, but it doesn't need to be. The point is to make your daily habit so easy to do that you never miss it. For example, maybe your exercise habit is to do 10 jumping jacks every morning. This is by no means a complete exercise regime, but if you have struggled to exercise daily, then starting with something this easy is doable for you every day. There is nothing in your life that makes you so busy that you cannot complete 10 jumping jacks.

What should you do if you miss a day?

Let's say something does go wrong and you miss a day. Don't worry, you're going to get out your calendar and make sure that the first thing you do tomorrow is to get back on track with your habit. Your motto should be *never miss two days*. That's it; you never, in your life, miss two days of your habit.[56]

This all may sound intense, but sainthood is intense!

Consider the stories of the saints. Did they live wishy-washy lives? No! They were all in. Wild horses couldn't keep them from praying every day.

Another way you can keep yourself accountable is to track your progress. Print off a blank month. If it's August, print off August. Just Google, "August calendar" for the year we're in. Hang it up, and every day that you start your morning off with prayer, put a big, red X on the day.

Do this every single day. As you create this winning streak, you won't want to stop.

We're requiring a high standard of consistency for your new habits, so start with something easy enough that you absolutely know you can do it. Make it easy to win. Don't initially start with something too ambitious, like praying for two hours per day. Start easy. You can do one minute of prayer every day. Over time, you can work up to half an hour in the morning and half an hour in the evening.

Set yourself up to win and gain momentum. If you only have to pray for one minute, or if you only have to exercise for two minutes, your anxiety will be low. You won't be stressed about getting it right. In the beginning, just focus on installing the new habit. It's fine if your prayer sounds awkward. It's fine if you do five measly push-ups on your knees and call it good for the day.

It's fine to suck at it, but it's not okay to skip it. For me, that includes writing. I write every single day, even if it's for a short period of time or I don't know what to write. I want to cultivate the habit of being a writer.

Embrace the process of creating new habits. While many books may claim you can instill a habit in as little as twenty days, some habits take longer – potentially up to two hundred and fifty days.[57] No matter how long the time required or how big the habit, you will go through three phases.

UNBEARABLE
Why did I decide to do this? This sucks! I want to give up! I'll never be able to do this. I always fail; I'm going to fail again!

UNCOMFORTABLE
I'm starting to see some benefits. I like what I'm seeing but it's still not fun. I don't like waking up early to pray but I think it's working.

UNSTOPPABLE
I feel great! I'm proud and I can really see the benefits. I'm not going to give up!

Go into this challenge knowing you'll live through these three phases. Being prepared to deal with the unbearable and uncomfortable phases will increase your chances of success. Habits are worth fighting for because they help free up our willpower to do other things.

The people who you admire for getting a lot done probably aren't using a lot of willpower for most of their daily routines. Instead, they've used their willpower to instill habits that have become effortless. Consider how many CEO's wear the same thing every day. They have so many mini-habits and routines built into their life that they are largely on autopilot. Their willpower is free to be focused on their most critical problems.

You have the most control over the first two hours of the day and the last two hours of the day. I suggest you try to put most of your good new habits in these two time slots.

I want you to be successful! I want you to feel like you have control over the first and last two hours of your day. Start thinking of the rhythms you want to create in your own life to make this possible. What's your STOP doing list and what's your START doing list? You're not going to work on it all at once. You may have to break down a habit into baby steps.

You can do this. You've got Jesus on your side.

Chapter Fourteen:
Be A Scientist

"This is the very perfection of a man, to find out his own imperfections."
– St. Augustine

I was never really into science in school. Chemistry was a chore; biology lost interest as soon as there weren't any more pictures of animals to look at, and running experiments always seemed a little annoying to me. I was much more into business. How does a company make money? How do you create a successful marketing plan? This got me excited.

Looking back now, I realize that I was actually….really into experiments; they were just marketing and financial experiments instead of chemical ones. Running experiments is about asking a question, gathering data, and seeing if the data answers your question. You have a problem, so you try a few solutions and see if something works. There is no emotion involved in experiments.

At the end of the day, a marketing campaign is successful or not, based on the numbers. A new medicine either decreases cancer cells or it doesn't. A water filtration system either cleans the water or it doesn't. A scientist does not attach emotions to these outcomes.

Failure to solve a problem may be frustrating, but we don't get angry at the data in the meantime. If we can apply this to our own lives and to the habits we're trying to instill, we will find that it becomes much easier to accept our successes and failures - and to change our behavior accordingly.

At one point in my marriage, I was frustrated that we were consistently going over our grocery budget. It had been three months, and I still didn't understand why. We had made a budget and a meal plan, and I was confident it would work out. Before the end of the month, however, the food was gone and our grocery budget had been eaten up. I felt so upset. I had a degree in finance, so why couldn't I make a simple grocery budget work?

I let myself give in to anger, bitterness, pouting, crying, guilt, and then hopelessness. In about two minutes I'll jump from "we blew our grocery budget," to "I'll never be a good housewife ever, for all time…and I'm going to be miserable."

It sounds pathetic, but it's easy for me to let the devil whisper lies and to believe them. What I see in the tirade above is a whole lot of feelings and not a lot of reasonable thinking. I remember accusing my husband of eating too much meat. Next, I was convinced we had lots of food we weren't using in the cupboards and that we must not buy anything for a week, eating the food in our cupboards instead.

In the end, after I was able to take a deep breath and separate my emotions from the problem, I decided to become a grocery scientist and to run an experiment. Instead of keeping track of what we were buying at the store and what was on my meal plan, I wrote down everything we were actually eating. What I discovered was, since we had stopped eating gluten, all four of us were eating more meat and fruit.

Guess what? Fruits and meats are expensive! Although I had been proud of my family's healthy eating habits, I didn't realize how it would significantly change the cost of what we were eating.

I found some inexpensive foods that I could substitute to get us closer to our budget. We fed the kids more rice and beans as a healthy and cheap alternative. I started increasing the amount of gluten-free carbs we were eating, including lots of sweet potatoes.

My husband and I discussed how to further reduce spending, and we agreed to try and cut back one-third of our meat consumption. Both he and I found that if we had a large piece of chicken on our plates, we'd eat it. Instead, if we put two-thirds of a piece of chicken there, we'd still be satisfied and would have more leftovers.

These aren't rocket scientist conclusions but since I had previously been so emotionally charged about the situation, I wasn't able to solve the problem. I wanted my family to eat healthy foods but I also wanted to be a good steward of our money. I let myself get upset and feel bad about my own shortcomings. Not only did I have a grocery budget problem, but I added a low self-esteem, grumpy mom problem as well!

Be a scientist. Check your emotions at the door and try to look at the data in front of you. Whether you're tackling money, health, marriage, or motherhood challenges, try to notice the cause and effect of what's going on in front of you. Don't get upset about it, just write down what you see.

It's All Just Data

Now it's your turn. What problems in your life feel so emotional that you are preventing yourself from finding a solution? If you're not losing weight, you might be tempted to beat yourself up and think the situation is hopeless. Instead, I want you to simply tell yourself, "That's some interesting data."

Sit down, unpack the last week like a non-emotional scientist, and figure out what happened. Maybe you can't eat bananas and still lose weight. Maybe you didn't drink enough water. Maybe you increased your strength training exercise, so you're building muscle.

If you and your husband suddenly seem snippy with each other, try to figure out why. When this happens to me, I try to take a deep breath, forget about what we argued about, and ask myself, *what happened this week*? Usually, I can find some unusual patterns that might be responsible for our bad moods. Maybe I haven't had any alone time in eight days. Maybe my husband has been working extra hours. Maybe we haven't had enough time together.

I try to act like a scientist and say, "That's some interesting data;" I wonder what I can do differently to produce a different outcome.

I do this with my children all the time! After we have a toddler meltdown, or if I notice that all of my children seem to be crying a lot, I instantly look for patterns. Instead of internalizing the lie that I'm a terrible mom who can't control her own children, I try to look for what led up to the tantrums.

It's usually one of a few things:

- They've had too much sugar;
- It's been too long since they've had healthy food;
- They've spent too much time in front of a screen;
- They are tired;
- I haven't spent enough uninterrupted, quality time with them;
- I'm not giving them enough positive feedback.

I used to get so upset on the days when nothing seemed to go right. I'd look up to God and say, "Why? How could this have been what you had planned for me? I'm terrible at raising small children!" You can see how quickly the devil uses these opportunities to get us to focus on ourselves and our own failings.

Take a deep breath, step back, and analyze your problem.

If you can keep your emotions checked, and look objectively at the hours or the week preceding the problem, you can usually find patterns. Journaling can be a big help to discover these patterns. It's difficult to remember the patterns in your life. When your write them down, however, you can recall things more easily and make connections more quickly.

"Oh, I see! When it's been raining for three-plus days and we're cooped up inside, the kids start to lose it."

With this realization, you may find the inspiration to build a fort, bake something special, or put on rain clothes and go for a rainy walk. You could easily have decided that you were a terrible mom with poorly behaved children. Alternatively, you could recognize the pattern and feel excited to solve it – even if you have to do something out of the ordinary.

This is the difference between reacting emotionally and being a scientist who looks at data.

Stop Being A Perfectionist

"To live is to change, and to be perfect is to
have changed often."
– Bl. John Henry Cardinal Newman

Perfectionism can be a very charged word. Some people even take pride in their perfectionism. Some may think of it as a dirty word that keeps us trapped, making you feel like you'll never live up to your own expectations. One of the reasons we feel so strongly about this word is that we think the alternative to being a perfectionist is to just let everything go.

If we have no standards, then we fear that everything will fall apart and we'll end up living in dirty houses with no food. We'll be late to everything and there will be great chaos! Yes, that does sound terrible. If I have to choose between chaos or perfectionism, I think I'd keep striving for perfection too!

I'm here to offer you an alternative. Instead of being a perfectionist, I want you to consider yourself an optimalist. Not an optimist, but an optimalist.[58] Let me explain.

When we're chasing perfection, we're constantly disappointed. We will never be perfect. The chase creates a constant state of failure. No wonder it feels bad!

A perfectionist sets her sight on something and refuses anything less than perfectly attaining her perfect target. Even when it becomes clear that this isn't the right thing to do, she clings to her idea, because to let it go would feel like a deep failure. She feels as if a small part of herself would die if she isn't perfect.

At the end of the day, perfectionists fail to allow for reality.

An optimalist, however, already knows that she will never be perfect. She may still have high expectations and big dreams, but she is able to account for reality as she chases her dreams. An optimalist is not scared of failure, and by letting go of the fear to fail, she has more freedom.

Brian Johnson says, "Life is a classroom, I'm going to make as many experiments as I possibly can."[59]

What's going to happen if your cake looks pathetic next to another mom's perfectly decorated one? If it's important, take some decorating classes. If it's not important, move on.

If you want to get better at something, take classes, watch YouTube videos, read a book, and get better. Failing at something once doesn't mean you're always destined to fail at it. I used to think I'd never get the hang of cleaning my house. I know that sounds silly, but I grew up in a two-bedroom apartment with a single mom who did everything after I went to sleep. I never had to learn how to clean and I thought I was incapable of it.

It was my choice to believe the lie, "I'll never know what I'm doing. It's all just too hard for me! I'll never be a good housekeeper."

Finally, I realized this wasn't who I wanted to be. I wanted to be better, and I had to learn how. I knew I would be learning how to take care of my house for the rest of my life. I took ownership of my situation. Now, I no longer feel like it's a huge personal failure if my house isn't perfect. It's just data, and I can choose to look at that data and make a new plan accordingly.

We need to stop trying so hard to look good. We must instead be committed to becoming better. A perfectionist cares about a magazine-like idea that she has in her head. When reality doesn't live up to expectations, she experiences a whole heap of negative emotions. An optimist says, "I want *this*." When it doesn't go according to plan, however, she says, "Okay, that needs work, so let's make a new plan."

Perfectionists tend to stay in their comfort zone because they're so afraid of failing. In the end, they keep themselves from the success they desire, because they are unwilling to try something new to get where they want to go. I think moms are particularly vulnerable to this type of thinking. They end up spinning their wheels for years on something that has a simple solution which they are simply unwilling to try.

I used to feel overwhelmed by the number of clothes my three daughters had. How could they own so many things? We had clothes for rain, snow, sunshine, and even second changes of clothes to put on after messes. We had tops that only matched one uniquely patterned skirt, and different colored shoes to go with all their church dresses.

I created this mountain of a clothes problem for myself by trying to have every possible clothing solution to any potential clothing situation.

This went on for a few years. Finally, I had to ask myself, "Who cares?" It seemed like this problem was mostly affecting me. My kids didn't care if their clothes matched or if they wore the same sweater a few days in a row. They didn't notice when I got rid of most of their dresses, leaving only two church dresses each.

My New and Improved Kid Clothing Plan:

- We got rid of all socks that weren't white.
- We kept silver church shoes (because they go with everything) and two church dresses.
- I got rid of all skirts and casual dresses. My girls always want to wear leggings, anyway, and then we didn't need tights anymore, except on Sundays.
- I rolled up six outfits for each of them in one drawer next to a basket of underwear. They could pick one pair of underwear and one "roll," which was a shirt and a pair of leggings.
- We did laundry on Mondays and Thursdays.
- I only kept clothes that all matched each other. I got rid of a lot of floral print stuff and neon-colored stuff that was hard to match.
- I kept a black sweater and a white sweater for each of them and put them away in the closet.
- All rain or snow gear went into a plastic container, also in the closet.

The particular system isn't important. What is important was that, as soon as I was able to set down my perfectionist ideals, I created a system that was easy to maintain and actually fun to use. Now I love every outfit my girls wear because I picked twelve pieces of clothing that match each other. We don't argue over socks. I have fewer clothes to wash and their room is less cluttered.

It has been great for me and my family, but I wouldn't have created this solution if I had remained fixated on always having perfectly dressed children.

Ladies, what I'm saying is you need to get over yourself. Put your ego in the corner for a minute and just be a scientist about what's not working in your life. Try to objectively figure out why it's not working and then go about finding a solution. Be willing to learn something new. Be willing to step outside your comfort zone.

When you're focused on getting better instead of looking good, the possibilities are endless. When a new system fails, it doesn't matter. It's good news because now you know and you can work on finding another system! You're going to be tweaking your life - for the whole rest of your life. Learn to embrace and enjoy the process!

Oh, The Seasons!

"Nothing appeases an enraged elephant so much as the sight of a little lamb."
—St. Francis de Sales

Many of us have heard "it's just a difficult season" as a fellow mom's excuse for not taking on a project or working on her health. Sometimes this is just an excuse we hide behind. Other times, however, there is a very valid reason for saying, "No." When you are pregnant and throwing up, you might just need to serve hot dogs for lunch every day.

My children don't watch a lot of TV. Sometimes, they get to watch a movie on Sunday. I'm proud that we keep our screen time to a minimum. When I'm pregnant, however, I have days where I'm a Netflix babysitting kind of mom.

During these times, it's important not to turn into a self-loathing, whiny mom because things aren't up to my normal standards.

When I'm having a bad spell, for whatever reason, I make peace with it from the beginning. It's important to manage expectations. If I'm thirty-seven weeks pregnant and I start a day expecting it to be amazingly productive, I'm likely to be disappointed. When I run out of energy at 10:30AM and am loading up Daniel Tiger for my kids to watch, I may feel like a big, fat failure.

When I take advantage of a good excuse to lower standards for longer than is really necessary, however, I often feel bad about myself, as I should. It's important to differentiate when you're genuinely in a bad season versus letting a small barrier be an excuse for not being responsible.

For example, I need easy-to-digest foods in my first trimester of pregnancy. That doesn't mean I need to get pasta from Olive Garden or start ordering cheese pizzas every day! I can choose simple rice or potatoes with butter instead. Deep down, I know when I am too self-indulgent.

If you're headed into a tough season or smack in the middle of one, make a deal with yourself. Decide what things you're going to let go and when you're going to pick them back up again. I remember letting my kids watch a lot more TV when I had a pinched nerve in my back at the end of my third pregnancy. I told myself that, after four weeks postpartum, we were turning it off again.

I created boundaries. I was giving myself permission to do something less than perfect, but only while I really required it.

You may occasionally need to do this with screen time, diet, house cleaning, etc. Some seasons are genuinely hard. Don't perpetually beat yourself up for lowering your standards during a hard season. Take control of the situation by acknowledging it and putting a definite end date to it. Now you can actually focus on what you need to.

Your Energy Tank (Eat, Move, Sleep)

"Don't you long to shout to those youths who are
bustling around you: Fools! Leave those worldly things
that shackle the heart – and very often degrade it – leave
all that and come with us in search of Love!"
– St. Josemaria Escriva

I know some of you might dread reading this chapter. Moms are notoriously bad at taking care of themselves. While we rush around making sure that everyone else is healthy and happy, we lack sleep, we don't eat well, and we keep putting off exercise.[60]

You need to keep your energy tank filled if you're going to take care of your husband, your children and all the other people God has put in your life. If your body is failing because you don't eat well, you don't sleep enough, or you aren't exercising, you're not going to be a good steward of those people. It will be difficult to strive for sainthood if your energy is depleted.

If you're tired or hungry, you're going to have much less willpower to tackle your to-do list. You'll be living as if you didn't charge your phone overnight, hoping to make it through the day with only 13% of your battery left.

What do you do when you only have 13% battery left on your phone? You shut down all the apps and use only what you absolutely must. Likewise, we have to take care of our body so that we have the energy to make good choices throughout the day. We don't want our willpower to become depleted.

I'm going to give you some tips for eating, moving and sleeping. As always, though, you want to be your own scientist and figure out what's best for you.

Eat

Let's start with food. We all have to eat. That's why emotional eating is one of the hardest addictions to kick. When you try to give up heroin, sure it's extremely painful, but you can put a bright line down and say, "I will never do heroin ever again!" You can't do that with food.

Food is everywhere, and you have to eat every single day. For moms, it's easy to forget this most basic human need.

There have been times when I get to 3 p.m. and I think, "Wow, I've had some coffee, an apple, and a Diet Coke today." That's bad. Although it's been a while since I've let myself do that, it's still easy to get so distracted that I forget to do basic things like eat healthy food throughout the day.

We have to stop eating like fifteen-year-olds.

Most of us know exactly what we need to *stop* eating and what we need to *start* eating. The first thing I would recommend tackling is sugar. I'm not talking about fruit here. I'm talking about refined sugar. It's pretty bad for you. We now consume more sugar in one day than most people annually consumed seventy-five years ago. Sugar is in everything now: you have to be a Sugar Ninja to kick it out of your life.

When we eat too much sugar or too many fried or fatty foods, we ride the blood sugar roller coaster. We zip up feeling giddy and full of weird energy, then we crash hard. We lose energy and we feel groggy, bloated, and weighed down. We're certainly not ready to tackle an afternoon with our kids during the witching hour.

It's like eating at Olive Garden. Sure, it sounds nice. But after eating a plateful of pasta (and really simple carbs like pasta are basically just sugar) and stuffing a few breadsticks down, I feel sick. I feel awful. I feel like sludge. Even now, in my mind, I think, "Mmm, Olive Garden." Those foods are so yummy when we eat them but they have bad consequences.

We have to stop lying to ourselves. This food is making us sick. It's not helping us become the best-version-of-ourselves.

Does that mean you can never go to Olive Garden? Of course not! We can still indulge in special treats. You cannot stay healthy, though, if you are frequently eating bad food (whether at home or at a restaurant.)

Here are some simple basic guidelines that apply to most of us:

> Eat more fresh, unprocessed foods (e.g. vegetables, fruit, nuts, coconut milk, meats and fish, etc. compatible with your nutritional restrictions)

> Eat fewer processed or modified foods (pizza, restaurant food, boxed food, bagged food, sugary foods, too much cheese, etc.)

It's not rocket science. Eating healthy is currently a matter of willpower for most of us. We need to instill healthy habits so our eating can become more automatic. Set yourself up for success by meal planning and being strong at the store. I don't have a lot of unhealthy food in my house because I don't buy unhealthy food at the store. I have more willpower walking through the aisles of a grocery store than at home.

When I get home, my willpower seems to vanish! If there are chocolate chips in my house, I will find them and eat them at the end of a bad day. The way I manage myself and my weakness is to not bring bad food home.

Some moms aren't tempted by the goldfish they buy for their kids. I am. I don't lie to myself and say, "I'm just buying this for the kids." I simply cannot have bad food in the house if I want to fight for my health.

Be honest with yourself. Set yourself up for success. You can do this. You can be healthy.

Your body depends on it. God has a great work he wants you to do, and you should be as healthy as you possibly can be so that you're ready to respond to His call.

Move

We all know we need to exercise. There is some form of exercise that each one of us is capable of doing. If you have a disability, find modified exercises that work for you. We need to move our bodies every day.

Here are some ways to help motivate you to exercise:

- Put on some upbeat music that you love to work out to;
- Schedule time to work out with a friend. If you can't work out together, at least keep each other accountable on your phone;
- Buy a FitBit, which tracks your exercise. There are lots of groups where you can share your information for more motivation;
- Do something with your spouse early in the morning before the kids wake up. I know that sounds difficult, but think of how you would feel if you exercised every single day first thing in the morning? You'd feel like a super woman!

I have three small children and a tight budget, so we do very simple things at home. I can't afford a gym membership. Furthermore, I don't want to make the time to drive to a gym, workout, and then drive home.

I have a twenty-five-pound kettlebell. If you google "kettlebell exercises," there are hundreds of them online. I work with my kettlebell in the morning. I do planks to strengthen my core. I do squats and push-ups throughout my day. And I try to get in 10,000 steps a day by zipping around my house and walking with my kids. This is doable for me.

Now am I in great shape? Not really. I want to be in better shape, but I'm working on different habits right now. Improving my health is in the queue, but it's not my main focus right now.

The important point is that you pick something and do it consistently. You can't continue to avoid exercise. Pick something you like, or that you can at least bear to do, and *do it*.

Sleep

Most Americans get fewer than six hours of sleep. Many of us are even prideful about this. "I can function with only five hours of sleep!" This is likely not true. You're certainly not at your best on five hours of sleep.

Getting a poor night of sleep is one of the biggest barriers that holds me back from being productive. That's why sleep was one of the first problems I focused on when I wanted to become a better version of myself.

My life improved noticeably when I started putting my phone away for good at 7:30 p.m., going to bed at 9:00 p.m., and waking up at 6:00 a.m.

This may sound crazy, but I didn't make all those changes overnight. I adopted them slowly.

My first step was to realize that I wasn't sleeping well. I was stretching out the nights after my kids went to sleep, hoping to relax and to finally have some time to myself or with my husband. I'd consistently get to bed at 10 or 11 p.m. feeling that the time had been wasted. I was too tired from the day to do anything meaningful, so that time was often spent watching TV.

I would check my phone compulsively throughout the night, letting email, Facebook, and Instagram pull my attention. I was mildly entertained but never fully focused. I even read books on my Kindle, and I'd read right up to the moment I prayed with my husband. We would turn out the light and go to sleep.

Except, I couldn't sleep. It would take me two hours to fall asleep, and it would be poor sleep.

Then one day I read about how bad blue screens are for our brains before bedtime. They mess with our circadian rhythms so that our bodies don't wind down naturally like they did hundreds of years ago.

The solution to my sleep issues started with cutting off all screen time at 7:30 p.m. That gave me an hour and a half to wind down before I wanted to go to sleep.

I'm not going to lie. It was tough to transition to this schedule.

I feared I was missing a crucial text or a timely email. What if someone posted something important? Even as I rattled off these worries in my head, I knew they weren't good reasons. I had become addicted to being plugged in, and I was experiencing withdrawals like an addict.

It took me three months to really let go of these feelings and find peace with unplugging at 7:30, ready to greet the online world again in the morning. This has been therapeutic for me. Not only has it been easier for me to fall asleep and to get deeper rest, but I also faced and overcame part of my digital addiction.

I am also very sensitive to caffeine, so I can't have coffee or any kind of caffeinated soda after 1 p.m. I can't eat chocolate after 5 p.m. I can't drink any alcohol before bed. For some reason, a glass of wine, while it makes me feel sleepy right after drinking it, keeps me awake for hours in the middle of the night. I have to be vigilant about not eating or drinking these things if I want to sleep well.

There are times when I make exceptions and have a piece of chocolate cake at an evening party. I do this knowing that I have to accept the consequences. I won't do this if I have to wake up rested and do something important the next day. I'm fully aware that these decisions will affect my sleep, and I own my choices.

Be a scientist. You, too, can figure out what helps you sleep well and what's getting in the way. Most importantly, you have to do it. You're an adult with a lot of responsibilities. You can't keep getting less sleep than what you need to be your best.

Breathe

"Love God, serve God; everything is in that."
– St. Clare of Assisi

We all have to breathe, but most of us are doing it wrong. It sounds silly. How can we be breathing wrong? Well, most of us are walking around taking panicky, shallow breaths most of the day. We are anxious and upset, and our bodies are constantly in a "fight or flight" state, often for hours. Our bodies were not designed to handle this amount of stress.

When you wake up in the morning and start worrying about your long list of things to do, your breathing becomes more rapid. Your body starts switching over to "I think there is a tiger in the grass over there" mode. You're triggering your "fight or flight" response by being overly worried about something that really isn't a big deal. It certainly isn't a tiger, so we don't need our bodies reacting accordingly as if it were.

The best way to combat our overreaction is to breathe deeply.

When you need to calm down, which I'm going to guess is at least three times an hour, this is how you should breathe.[61]

Breathe in through your nose for six seconds
Hold your breath for two seconds
Breathe out through your mouth – 7 seconds

You will immediately get more oxygen to your brain, and you will calm down. Stop seeing tigers everywhere. Life is not that big of a deal. You need to work on remaining calm. Stop flooding your body with adrenaline that you don't need. You're slowly wrecking your body.

We need to work on breathing well all throughout the day. Put a sticky note in your car. My mom has a great phrase written on a yellow sticky note in her car that says, "Breathe in His grace, breathe out His praise." This is a wonderful way to remember to breathe and praise our Lord at the same time! It may sound surprising, but working on your breathing will help you have a more peaceful and productive day.

Productive Procrastination

In college, my room was never so clean as it was during finals week. I still have the tendency to be very productive in non-essential areas of my life, when I should be focused on something more important. I'm really good at reorganizing my bills and our finances when I should be focusing on cooking healthy food. I have often been found sorting every single piece of clothing in our entire household when I should be making progress on our homeschooling curriculum.

Learn how to spot productive procrastination. This occurs when you focus on something that is good but not crucial. It's easy to hide behind productive procrastination because it usually involves doing something that seems important like cleaning, reading with the children, organizing, etc. When we do these activities, however, instead of the more important items on our task list, we are not being good stewards.

We are not being responsible when we stick with comfortable work to avoid the hard or uncomfortable things we're responsible for.

Because productive procrastination still looks like work, it can be hard to identify. It really comes down to clearly identifying your priorities. You'll often have an uneasy feeling when you're working on the wrong thing while you let a more important task go unfinished. You won't have the same sense of "job well done" because you know, deep down, that you're doing it for the wrong reason.

The best way to overcome this is to regularly check in with your weekly and monthly plans. Look for something that you're avoiding. Take some quick notes about why you're avoiding it.

- Is there a conversation you don't want to have?
- Will it be physically hard to do this task?
- Is it emotionally draining to do the work you need to do?
- Does it involve a person you don't want to interact with?
- Will the activity be boring?

Acknowledge whatever yucky feelings you have about this task. Go back to the Motivation Equation if you need to remember why this task was initially important to you. Finally, see if you can create a game by setting a timer or doing something special when you're done, like taking a bubble bath.

Sometimes we have hard and uncomfortable things we just need to do. Say a prayer to St. Maximillian Kolbe and ask for the strength to do the hard work for Jesus. Offer up your suffering to Mary. Then get to work. You're an adult and you can handle this!

Chapter Fifteen:
When It All Goes Wrong
(Because It Will)

It would be naive of us to assume that after reading one book, your life will suddenly go smoothly without any bumps. God does not promise us a life without storms. Rather, He promises that we can have peace even when we're in the middle of a terrible crisis. It's hard to cultivate peace in times of trouble, but it's absolutely possible. One of the ways we can manage difficult situations better is to have a plan in place for how to deal with them when they occur.

We're going to talk about what to do when you and your spouse aren't on the same page. This can be painful and, when our marriage is struggling, we often don't see clearly.

We'll cover how you can prioritize your life when you feel like everything is falling apart. What should your first steps be when you feel paralyzed?

We'll also talk about how to move forward when you've crashed and burned. How many of us have started a program with great enthusiasm only to let it fade into the background as we get distracted with what's around us?

I don't want this to happen, but if it does, let's make sure we have a plan to get you back on track.

Don't be discouraged when you read this section. Find hope in the idea that when a rough patch comes, you'll be prepared. It's why I believe the Catholic Mom Challenge system really works for every Catholic mom! It's flexible and it survives the test of a less-than-perfect life.

When You and Your Husband Aren't On the Same Page

Let's be honest, it can be really difficult to make progress in any area of your life if you and your spouse don't agree. This can be emotional, painful and oftentimes confusing. When should we honor what our husband says and when should we insist our opinion is considered?

Since I converted to Protestantism, I have been a fan of the *husband leads a household* way of thinking. God designed marriage to work with spouses who operate as a team and a husband who acts as the captain of the team. In many Catholic marriages, however, husbands are unwilling to act as that captain. Some husbands do take on this role but execute it poorly without wisdom. And some husbands never get the chance to be the leader of their family because their wives are firmly entrenched in that role and won't give it up.

This is certainly not the book to solve complex marriage issues. As always, though, I will challenge you to be realistic about your situation. Try to take a few steps back and ask yourself what's going on. Why are you two not on the same page?

As my husband often says, "All marriage problems are caused by both spouses." There may be different levels of fault, but we are a team. We are one flesh and every issue we face is caused by both of us in some way. Sometimes I am too upset to hear this or to process it, especially if I feel wronged or unappreciated by him. Get to a place where you are calm and then try to figure out what you're doing that's contributing to your issues.

If you and your husband aren't on the same page about a particular issue or many issues, here are some things you should avoid doing and some tips for what you can do instead:

DON'T give him this book. This book is not intended for men. He will likely be offended and not read the book at all. You won't make much progress.

DO give him a copy of *Be A Man*[62] or *Catholic Manhood Today*.[63] It's even better if you can get a friend to recommend these books. Some husbands don't like being told what to read and won't value the suggestion if it comes from their wife, especially if you're in a time of tension.

DON'T try and solve all your problems by yourself if you're deeply entrenched. Marriage is personal – we often don't get help because we are embarrassed. Spouses are often so deeply intertwined that they need a third party to help find clarity.

DO talk to a priest or get counseling. This can seem awkward and uncomfortable, but your marriage is worth suffering for. Sometimes a calm and experienced person can bring wisdom to help you make progress.

DON'T go rogue. When a husband is unwilling to cooperate, it can be tempting to throw up your hands and do everything on your own and in your own way. Don't fall into this trap. Of course, you need to still take care of your family, pay your bills and keep living forward, but you don't need to thumb your nose at him with decisions you know he doesn't agree with. Don't let revenge and malice live in your heart.

DO write out your plans (i.e. creating a budget, schooling for the kids, housecleaning or spiritual growth.) Show how you've been thoughtful about his needs by creating a plan that incorporates what he wants. Ask him to review and help you change those plans so he feels part of the process. Tell him you'll put a time limit on this discussion so he's not afraid of walking into a three-hour long conversation.

DON'T use your husband as an emotional dumpster. Many wives feel like they have permission to dump all their emotions on their husbands without filtering out the lies and exaggerations.

DO try to compose yourself and limit how many words you use to describe how you're feeling and what you're going through. He will be much more likely to help you if he doesn't feel like you're monopolizing the time he's making to sit down and talk with you. Be efficient.

Regardless of your husband's reaction, your God-given task is to serve him and to love him. I know this is hard for many of us to hear. You are more likely to win his heart to your cause through humility than with a harsh word. This isn't an excuse to stay in an abusive relationship or to be a doormat.

Many of us are so worried that our husbands are going to steamroll us that we jump in before they have the chance. Give your husband an opportunity to really love you. Approach him gently and you may be surprised that he will open up.

How to Prioritize When it ALL Feels Important

There are seasons when every area of our lives seem to be falling apart. We feel like we're being attacked on multiple fronts: marriage, finances, health, homemaking, and motherhood. We're drowning and we don't know where to begin.

This is a very difficult reality for some of you right now. I want you to take a deep breath and step back from the many fires that are burning. I'm hoping to help you put things in order.

When my life feels crazy, the first thing I ask myself is, "How is my spiritual life?"

If I have been neglecting my Bible reading, the first thing I do is find my Bible and put it on my nightstand. I make it a point to read it in the morning and in the evening. I will pick the Psalms, Proverbs or go through the gospels. I personally like the book of James and Sirach too.

Make sure you're setting aside time to pray every day. If possible, go to Adoration once a week. If you haven't been to Confession in a while, schedule that immediately. These are always the first things I turn to when I am in crisis. It may seem out of order to make time for these things, but that's how God's economy works. He will honor the time you spend drawing closer to Him. He will give you grace and strength to tackle the rest of your challenges.

Remember what Jesus said to Martha, "My dear Martha, you are anxious and troubled about many things, but one thing is necessary. Mary has chosen what is better, and it will not be taken away from her." Luke 10:41-42[64] In the Latin translation, Mary has chosen not only something "better", but instead the "unum necessarium" or "only thing that is actually necessary." If you are not spending time with the Lord then your priorities are unbalanced.

After you have made a plan to get prayer and Bible reading back into your daily schedule, it's time to evaluate everything else that's on your plate.

You need to understand the "Eisenhower Method"[65] for organizing tasks. Dwight D. Eisenhower evaluated his tasks based on how urgent and important they were. He used four quadrants known as the Eisenhower Matrix. Here is how tasks are handled according to this model:

1. Important/Urgent tasks are done immediately and personally.
2. Important/Not Urgent tasks get a definite end date and are done personally.
3. Unimportant/Urgent tasks are delegated
4. Unimportant/Not Urgent tasks are dropped

Here is an example of items that would be in each category:

	Urgent	Not Urgent
Important	Crying baby Kitchen fire Some calls	Exercise Vocation Planning
Not Important	Interruptions Distractions Some calls	Trivia Busy work Time Wasters

66

When I'm in what I call "hair burning on fire" mode, when everything feels urgent and I'm overwhelmed with all the things that need to be done, I go through the following steps to prioritize my to-do list. I try to limit this planning session to only ten to fifteen minutes.

1. Make a list of all the tasks that need to be done and all the problems I'm having.

2. Assign a quadrant to each item using the Eisenhower Matrix above.
3. List all the Important/Urgent items on a separate sheet of paper. This helps me to see how small the Needs To Be Done Now list actually is.
4. I ask myself which tasks will be easier if I do a different one first. For example, if my husband and I are fighting, it will be hard for me to make progress on creating a budget for the family. I need to work on resolving issues with my husband first before tackling money issues.
5. Identify important tasks that take two minutes or less and I get those done immediately. Since it takes more than two minutes to worry about small tasks, it's more efficient to get them out of the way.
6. Delegate anything from quadrant three, if possible. Delay or discard tasks, if necessary.
7. List the top five things from quadrant one (or quadrant two if there are less than five things in quadrant one) and I schedule a time to do them.

Though I try to keep this activity to ten to fifteen minutes, sometimes I take longer – especially if I need to vent and get everything out of my head. Doing this also highlights how silly I am to worry about small things that don't really matter. This process helps me to acknowledge that I have been anxious over things I don't need to be anxious about. For me, the writing process itself can be very therapeutic.

I have a video on my website to walk you through this processing using actual examples so you can see how to make tough decisions and move forward with your top priorities.

Don't be afraid to ask for help. If family can't help you, reach out to your church. We have a beautiful faith and a community that often steps up when asked. Let your community know that you are struggling and see if someone will help you. It can be humbling to do this, but it's necessary. Again, I'll recommend *On The Other Side of Fear* by Hallie Lord.[67] She has lived through some incredibly difficult times, yet still managed to hang on to Jesus throughout them.

Just Resume

"It was pride that changed angels into devils; it is humility that makes men as angels."
– Saint Augustine

Before this system, I did not know how to effectively manage habits. I would try to instill a new habit into my daily routine, but when I missed a day, I'd respond, "Oh well, I guess it's over; I give up!" It sounds childish, but it's easy for anyone to do this – especially if the new habit is a little outside of our comfort zone. We're looking for a reason to give up.

What if the situation gets really bad? Perhaps you've blown it for weeks or even months. You've gained fifteen pounds, you stopped exercising, past due bills have been shoved in a desk drawer somewhere, you're living on four-and-a-half hours of sleep, and you don't even know where your Bible is.

Pull out your Catholic Mom Manifesto. If you lost it, print it again. If your printer (like most printers) is broken, then ask a friend to print it or go print it at the library. It's not very long.

Read your Stewardship Statements and Mission Statements. See what amazing things God has made you a steward of. Read about your vision for each life facet. Read all the plans you once made and thought were important.

"Do not dig up in doubt what you planted in faith." – Elizabeth Elliot[68]

Now, review the Motivation Equation again. For each plan you dropped, was it really important to you? Did you have unrealistic expectations? Did you give yourself enough time?

If possible, go to Confession and spend an hour in Adoration. If that's not possible right away, just get in a quiet space and pray. Read your Bible if you can. I love going back to the book of James. This book of the Bible is my anchor. When I'm feeling desperate and hopeless, there's something about reading the Letter of James that always reaches me. Since I've become Catholic, the book of Sirach has also become a favorite for helping to lift me out of my bad spot.

Here's the most important step: just resume.[69]

Don't make a big deal out of it. Don't beat yourself up. Don't worry about the future. You've gone through the work of creating your Catholic Mom Manifesto: you've done the hard part. Now just resume. Get back on track. Start doing the good things and stop doing the bad things.

It really is that simple. Sometimes we think we need a new, grand program to help us. Most of the time, however, we need to stop being petulant teenagers and just resume being an adult. The phrase "just resume" comes from Susan Thompson, who developed an awesome (though very expensive) weight loss program called *Bright Lines*[70], and I think this phrase is lovely.

Just resume.

It's so smooth. You can do it. Just move forward and be better. What has happened in the past does not determine your future. You may have failed one hundred times already, but that doesn't mean you're going to fail again. It's your job to be a scientist and try to figure out what's not working. If your target is reasonable and attainable, then just resume.

Signs I'm Out Of Tune

"He who climbs never stops going from beginning to beginning, through beginnings that have no end. He never stops desiring what he already knows."
–St. Gregory of Nissa

It's important that you are able to recognize when things are going wrong. Let's say your Catholic Mom Manifesto was left on the floor of your car. You've gotten busy and stopped following the program. Your schedule is filling up, you're frazzled and, you're letting the world tell you what's important again. Don't worry; this happens to all of us at some point.

When I'm in a calm and happy place, I make a list of big red flags that help alert me that I've gone off plan. These red flags are usually bad behaviors of mine that reveal I'm not being the best version of myself.

I added my list of big red flags near the back of my Catholic Mom Manifesto. I try to read them often, so I can be on the lookout for signs that my heart is out of tune. Here is a list of ten big red flags that tell me I need more Jesus in my life:

- I snap at my children out of impatience and anger;
- I soothe my stress by eating unhealthy food and I eat it too quickly;
- I don't stick to my prayer routines;
- I focus on what my husband can do for me instead of what I could do for him;
- I daydream about buying a new house, getting a puppy, or starting a new business because I'm looking for something shiny and distracting;
- I put off working on my ministry to watch television online;
- I stop showering and start to wallow in sadness. (This is a big red flag that I'm depressed and it usually coincides with a lack of prayer and sacraments in my life;)
- I allow the house to get dirty and cluttered, not because I'm busy, but because I don't feel like doing anything;

- I stay home for more than five days without seeing anyone except my family.

I don't need to hear the booming voice of God to know that snapping at my children is not the best-version-of-myself. When I notice myself doing the things on the list above, these actions are like road marks that tell me I am off course. I need to recommit to prayer, reading my Bible, monthly Confession, and praying the Rosary. Those are the tools I use to get back on track and to be the person God is calling me to be.

Don't let your pride derail you.

When I get too focused on myself, I try to remember this quote from St. Vincent de Paul:

> *"The most powerful weapon to conquer the devil is humility. For, as he does not know at all how to employ it, neither does he know how to defend himself from it."*
> *-Saint Vincent de Paul*[71]

Be humble. Confess your brokenness to God. We are weak, and our flesh makes us sinful. I don't think any of us can truly comprehend what we suffer because of Original Sin. Take your failings and your sin to the foot of the Cross. Lay them there and ask God to forgive you. Ask Him to give you strength. We will have to keep doing this for the rest of our lives.

We're at the end of the program, and I've put you through a lot of tough love. I'm proud of you for making it through. Before I end, however, I'd like to leave you with some encouragement.

Conclusion:
Girl, You Got This

I believe in you. More than that, God believes in you. He is your Abba Father, smiling down on you right now. He's thinking, "There she is, that amazing woman. I love her just the way I created her." God's heart is full of love for you. He is so proud of your efforts toward sanctification even when you have stumbled and made mistakes.

I believe one of the gifts of motherhood is that we get a glimpse of the unconditional love that God has for us through the way we love our children. Of course, it drives us nuts when our kids make bad choices, but that never affects our deep love for them. Raising our children gives us a very tiny view of how God looks at us.

He loves you so much. He has a specific plan for you here on Earth. He wants you to strive for sainthood. He wants you to do the good work that He has planned for you.

God knows the right combination of suffering and success that will lead you to Heaven. It's your job to detach yourself from the world, get in tune with Him, and discern what His plan is – then do it.

I want you to take the time and create a Catholic Mom Manifesto. I want you to join the Catholic Mom Challenge Facebook group and make some friends. I want you to surround yourself with people who love you and want to challenge you to become the best-version-of-yourself.

God's intent for you is to live a life without fear, anxiety, or anger. I know that's a tall order, but when we walk with the Lord, when we make Jesus Christ the center of our life, our lives will be more peaceful. This is worth fighting for. More than that, it's the life God is asking, and inviting us, to live.

He wants us to learn to detach ourselves from worldly desires and to strive for sainthood. Our path will be unique, but He will give us the grace to walk our specific path.

I want you to weave prayer and the sacraments throughout your week so that you can refresh your soul, fill up your spiritual and emotional energy, and live out your mission. Thank you for reading the Catholic Mom Challenge and for being part of what I hope will be a movement among Catholic moms. My hope is that Challengers will pop up in every parish and work to inspire each other to strive for sainthood!

Next Steps

To get started with the Catholic Mom Challenge system, visit www.CatholicMomChallenge.com and download the worksheets. Follow the instructions and watch the videos if you want some extra help along the way. On this website, I also list dozens of book recommendations and resources that I have found to be helpful.

If you want to follow me along my own journey, you can sign up to be on my Challengers email list, where I send a quick 2-3 lines of something inspirational every day!

If you want some extra help and accountability, sign up for a Catholic Mom Challenge online workshop. The first workshop will be available January 2017. You can read more details about this program on my website.

Join the Catholic Mom Challenge Facebook group at www.facebook.com/groups/catholicmomchallenge where you can meet Catholic moms who are striving for sainthood, just like you. This is a nice crowd and a place where you can ask for advice, get feedback or just make some friends!

I never get tired of meeting people and hearing their story. Email me at letschat@sterlingjaquith.com. It may take me a bit, but I will respond. I especially love to hear conversion stories and stories about how you met your husband!

Thank You

Before I wrote a single word of this book, I sat in Adoration and I prayed. I prayed that the Holy Spirit would give me the words you needed to hear. I sat for a long time until I picked up my pencil and wrote down the words I heard in my heart. I will not pretend to know the will of God or what He would say to you but here are the words I wrote in Adoration that day:

> Dear Daughter of Mine,
>
> I love you. You are a treasure to me. Oh, how I wish you would treasure yourself as I treasure you. You are perfect because I made you to be perfect. I placed you on Earth at precisely this time. You have a great work to do that only you can do.
>
> I will tell you what I want you to do when you spend time with me, so do this often. Visit me in your prayers and come visit me in Adoration. I am always waiting for you. Close your eyes and ears to the world and open your heart to me. I will give you purpose, guidance, support and most of all, love.
>
> Daughter, I know you need to be loved more than anything. I will always love you.
>
> My mother loves you too. She is waiting for you to run into her arms. Cry on her shoulder and let her be your mother. She will give you comfort. She can sweeten your trials and she will pray for you every time you ask.
>
> Be anxious for nothing. Embrace all your suffering, large and small. This way you will come to know my sacrifice for you and you may share in the redemption of others. Yes, your suffering matters but only if you give it to me in your heart.
>
> Be strong, my daughter. More than ever, I need you to be a light in the world. Shine your light in the darkness and spread love wherever you go. Be kind to your husband and your children. Do not let anger steal your joy.

I am your father and I want to spend eternity with you. Choose Heaven over the world you live in. Your time there is short, so run to me with open arms, keeping your eyes fixed on me. I will fulfill your heart's desire and bring you peace.

Spend time with me every day and I will show you how to stay on the right path and I will give you the strength to walk it.

Peace Always,

Your Father In Heaven

Thank you for taking the time to read this book. I created this program out of love. It is from this love that I send you out into the world armed with this new information about how you can strive for sainthood, right now, with the life God has given you. Your own salvation is your hands.

It's hard for me to finish this paragraph because I don't want it to be over. But just as I love Mondays and the New Year, I love new beginnings. Let the end of this book be a new beginning for you. Take charge of your life by first giving it all over to Christ. Then follow His lead and strive for sainthood with every ounce of energy you have. We're fighting for eternity. Let's fight alongside each other as women, as wives, as mothers and as daughters of the one true King.

> *"Let us begin in earnest to work out our salvation, for no one will do it for us, since even He Himself, Who made us without ourselves, will not save us without ourselves." -*
> *St. Margaret Mary Alacoque*

Acknowledgements

I have to thank the Lord for putting this desire in my heart to write a book for Catholic moms. Thank you for giving me the grace and strength to see it through.

I want to thank my amazing husband for tirelessly supporting me by cooking meals, watching the children, reading many versions of this book and being my cheerleader throughout this process. I want to thank my mom and her husband for living with us and loving my children. Multi-generational living can be tough but it's a huge blessing! I want to thank all my friends who answered my seemingly endless questions. Thank you, Jeannie Ewing, for editing my book and teaching me about the proper use of commas!

I want to thank Fr. Peter Arteaga and Fr. Ben Uhlenkott for their constant inspiration. You both radiate love everywhere you go. I see Christ shining through you. Your commitment to your vocation inspires me!

I want to thank all the men and women who pour their hearts into Catholic ministry. It's hard to balance home life with this type of work but it's absolutely needed. Specifically, Gregory Popcak, Lisa Hendy, Matthew Kelly, George Weigel, Sherry Weddell, Scott and Kimberly Hahn and Katie Warner - your books have fed me, encouraged me and given me hope. Thank you for all that you do!

And lastly to all the women who read my blog, listen to my Coffee & Pearls podcast, and who interact with me on Facebook, Instagram, and Twitter – you are my friends. You are the reason I keep writing even when it's tough. Your emails and your stories bring me joy. Your lives have changed mine and I thank you from the bottom of my heart for the community we share.

Can You Do Me A Favor?

Thank you for reading my book!

If you have any feedback or if you'd like to share how this book has affected you, please email me at letschat@sterlingjaquith.com.

If you could take a moment and leave me a review on Amazon, I would really appreciate it! New authors rely on reviews so readers will give them a chance.

Thank you again for being part of the Catholic Mom Challenge. I hope you enjoyed reading this book as much I enjoyed writing it!

Appendix A

Spirituality Questions

Are you setting aside time to pray daily?

Have you gone through Marian consecration?

Do you do a Daily Examination of Conscience at the end of the day?

Do you read your Bible every day?

Are you attending Mass every Sunday?

How often are you going to Adoration?

When was the last time you went to Confession?

Do you have a spiritual advisor?

Are there local Bible studies you could attend?

Do you have Catholic books you are reading?

Do you have a copy of the Catechism?

Do you know what a novena is? When is the last time you prayed one?

Do you have a patron saint? How often do you pray to your patron saint?

Have you read any books about the doctors of the church?

Do you have a Rosary? How often do you pray the Rosary?

Do you pray the Divine Mercy Chaplet?

Do you know what the seven deadly sins are?

Do you know what the cardinal virtues are?

Have you memorized the Apostles Creed?

How are you bringing faith into your family life?

How are you bringing faith into your marriage?

Are you living life with the rhythms of the Liturgical calendar (i.e. celebrating feast and fasts?)

Do you have a prayer journal?

Do you pray when eating out, or are you embarrassed?

Do people who meet you know that you are Catholic?

Do you feel comfortable and confident discussing your faith with friends, family, and neighbors?

Do you know and understand the Creed?

Marriage Questions

Are you praying every day for your spouse?

Do you and your spouse pray together, out loud, at least once per day?

Do you have a weekly or monthly planning session where you and your husband get on the same page about priorities and schedules?

Are you prioritizing your children, your job or your family above your husband?

Are you prioritizing your husband above your relationship with Jesus?

Do you have a weekly date night?

Have you made a list of 25 things you can do to show your spouse you love him?

Do you know your husband's love language?

Do you know your husband's temperament?

Do you know your husbands Myers-Briggs personality type?

Do you think you need spiritual counseling or marriage counseling to help your marriage?

Could you join a marriage Bible study or a local Teams of Our Lady group?

Have you forgiven your spouse for anything he may have done to you in the past?

Do you have bitterness in your heart about some aspect of your marriage?

How is your intimate life? If it's not great, how can you improve it?

Are you using Natural Family Planning and if so, are there more resources you could look into to make this easier on your marriage?

Is it time to read a Catholic book about marriage?

In what ways are you sabotaging your marriage?

Do you and your husband act like a team or are you living more like roommates?

How can you be more respectful of your husband?

Are you prioritizing physical intimacy with your husband?

Do you sometimes withhold physical intimacy to manipulate your husband?

When is the last time you went away for the weekend alone with your spouse?

Do you regularly look for opportunities to serve your spouse?

Motherhood Questions

What areas of your parenting are you not being consistent about?

Do you have peace about your vocation as a mother?

Do your children see you pray?

Am I teaching my children to value learning?

Am I teaching my children virtues?

Am I role modeling virtues for my children?

Am I teach my children to value hard work?

Am I teaching my children to live out their faith?

How do you incorporation Catholicism in your children's lives outside of Mass?

Do you pray for each of your children specifically?

Do you pray for their future vocation and spouses?

Which aspects of me am I afraid my children will adopt?

Which aspects of me do I hope my children will adopt?

Do you apologize to your children when you're wrong?

Are your children helping out enough around the home?

Do I praise my children enough?

Am I parenting out of fear or comfort?

Do I discipline my child with love?

Do you spend quality one-on-one time with your children?

Are you feeding your children healthy food?

Do you encourage your children to exercise regularly?

Are you preparing your children adequately to be independent adults?

Do you spend time reading out loud to your children?

Do you encourage your children to read?

Are you limited screen time?

Do you know who your children spend time with?

Who influences your children outside of the home? Are you okay with that influence?

Do you yell too often at your children?

Are you most often anxious and in a hurry when you're around your children?

Do you celebrate feast days with your children?

Rest Questions

Am I getting enough time to recharge my batteries?

Do I really consider that rest is important and will improve my other facets?

Do I actually make time for rest or do I just use my free time for fun activities?

Are my "rest" activities genuinely restful or are they harmful (i.e. watching blue screens before bed.)

Do I need to ask for support from my spouse, friends, or family to get more rest?

Is my husband committed to helping me find genuine rest?

If not, have I discussed the need with him (and helped discuss his need as well)?

What are some activities that help me genuinely recharge?

Do I need to make time for rest in the mooring or the evening when I have more control over my time?

Am I making poor excuses for not getting the rest I need?

Am I putting everyone else's health and rest before my own?

Can I find ways to rest with my spouse?

Can I find ways to rest with a friend?

Can I find ways to rest with my children?

Is there a place I can go that I find peaceful?

Do I find reading, gardening, knitting or some other hobby to be restful?

What obligations do I need to let go of so I can find more time to recharge?

Finance Questions

Do you have a budget?

Are you sticking to your budget?

Do you and your husband regularly review your budget?

Are you and your husband (generally) in agreement about the details of the budget.

Have you and your husband gone through Dave Ramsey's program or something similar?

Have you gone back and looked at your last six months of spending to know where your money is going?

Do you know how much debt you owe?

Do you know the interest rate for every piece of debt you have?

Are you saving money for retirement?

Do you have a savings account? If yes, do you regularly put money in it?

Do you pay attention to how much money you spend on food?

Do you put money away for common expenditures (e.g. car repair, vacations, presents etc.?)

Do you need a financial advisor?

Are you and your husband on the same page about your financial plan?

Who is responsible for paying your bills?

Can you set some of your bills up to autopay?

Can you pay your house off more quickly?

What things can you do to make more money?

Can you sell some things at a garage sale?

Health Questions

Are you eating healthy food?
If you don't know, are you willing to find out what healthy food is?
Are you getting enough exercise?
Do you drink enough water?
Do you consume too much alcohol, sugar or fat?
Are you taking any powerful drugs without a prescription?
Are you setting a good example of health for your children?
When is the last time you went to the doctor or OBGYN for a check up?
Do you have a healthy blood pressure?
Are you a healthy weight for your height and body type?
Should you be taking vitamins?
Have you ever had your thyroid levels checked?
Do you use natural family planning?
When is the last time you went to the dentist? Do you floss regularly?
When do you feel bloated, have headaches or bathroom issues etc.?)
Are you trying to solve this problem?
Are there certain foods that cause you allergic reactions?

Homemaking Questions

Are you happy with your homemaking systems?
Do you have a chore chart?
Could your children do more chores?
Are you being a perfectionist about how things are done or can you lower your standards so your family can help you?
Do you and your husband discuss what each of your house duties?
Do you have a meal plan?
Do you try to prepare nutritious food for your family?
Do you cultivate an atmosphere of peace in your home?
Can you embrace minimalism and get rid of some of your stuff?
Could you have a garage sale to minimize your clutter?
What cleaning routines do you need to get better at?
Are you being kind to your children and your husband?
Do you have one space where you can sit, relax and read your Bible?
Do you have a sacred space in your home where your family can pray?

Appendix B

Spirituality Quotes:

Be on your guard; stand firm in the faith; be courageous; be strong. 1 Corinthians 16:13

Who is it that overcomes the world? Only the one who believes that Jesus is the Son of God. 1 John 5:5

I have been crucified with Christ and I no longer live, but Christ lives in me. The life I now live in the body, I live by faith in the Son of God, who loved me and gave himself for me. Galatians 2:20

For God so loved the world that he gave his one and only Son, that whoever believes in him shall not perish by have eternal life. John 3:16

Whoever believes in the Son has eternal life, but whoever rejects the Son will not see life, for God's wrath remains on them. John 3:36

Then Jesus declared, "I am the bread of life. Whoever comes to me will never go hungry, and however believes in me will never be thirsty. John 6:35

May the God of hope fill you with all joy and peace as you trust in him, so that you may overflow with hope by the power of the Holy Spirit. Romans 15:13

Do not be conformed to this world, but be transformed by the renewing of your mind, that you may prove what the will of God is, that which is good and acceptable and perfect. Romans 12:2

For we live by faith, not by sight. 2 Corinthians 5:7

In the hope of eternal life, which God, who does not lie, promised before the beginning of time. Titus 1:2

Ignorance of scripture is ignorance of Christ. – St. Jerome

If you believe what you like in the gospels, and reject what you don't like, it is not the gospel you believe, but yourself. St. Augustine

The Holy Bible is like a mirror before our mind's eye. In it we see our inner face. From the Scriptures we can learn our spiritual deformities and beauties. And there too we discover the progress we are making and how far we are from perfection. – Pope St. Gregory

At the end of our life, we shall be judged by charity. St. John of the Cross

If there be a true way that leads to the Everlasting Kingdom, it is most certainly that of suffering, patiently endured. St. Colette

Let us therefore give ourselves to God with a great desire to begin to live thus, and beg Him to destroy in us the life of the world of sin, and to establish His life within us. – St. John Eudes

You must ask God to give you power to fight against the sin of pride which is your greatest enemy – the root of all that is evil, and the failure of all that is good. For God resists the proud." St. Vincent de Paul

You cannot please both God and the world at the same time. They are utterly opposed to each other in their thoughts, their desires, and their actions." St. John Vianney

We become what we love and who we love shapes what we become. If we love things, we become a thing. If we love nothing, we become nothing. Imitation is not a literal mimicking of Christ, rather it means becoming the image of the beloved, an image disclosed through transformation. This means we are to become vessels of God's compassionate love for others. St. Clare of Assisi

All of us can attain to Christian virtue and holiness, no matter in what condition of life we live and no matter what our life work may be. -Saint Francis de Sales

It is simply impossible to lead, without the aid of prayer, a virtuous life. - Saint John Chrysostom

Marriage Quotes:

Love is patient and kind; love is not jealous or boastful; it is not arrogant or rude. Love does not insist on its own way; it is not irritable or resentful; it does not rejoice at wrong, but rejoices in the right. Love bears all things, believes all things, hopes all things, endures all things. 1 Corinthians 13:4-7

A wife of noble character is her husband's crown, but a disgraceful wife is like decay in his bones. Provers 12:4

Houses and wealth are inherited from parents, but a prudent wife is from the Lord. Proverbs 19:14

A wife of noble character who can find? She is worth far more than rubies. Probers 31:10

Wives, submit yourselves to your husbands, as is fitting in the Lord. Husbands, love your wives and do not be harsh with them. Colossians 3:18-19

Marriage is to help married people sanctify themselves and others. For this reason they receive a special grace in the sacrament which Jesus Christ instituted. Those who are called to the married stat will, with the grace of God, find within their state everything they need to be holy. Saint Josemaria Escriva

Spread love everywhere you go: first of all in your own house. Give love to your children, to your wife or husband, to a next door neighbor... Let no one ever come to you without leaving better and happier. Be the living expression of God's kindness; kindness in your face, kindness in your eyes, kindness in your smile, kindness in your warm greeting. – Blessed Mother Teresa of Calcutta

You learn to speak by speaking, to study by studying, to run by running, to work by working, and just so, you learn to love by loving. All those who think to learn in any other way deceive themselves. St. Francis de Sales

"The union of man and woman in marriage is a unique, natural, fundamental and beautiful good for persons, communities, and whole societies. Pope Frances

The love of husband and wife is the force that welds society together – St. John Chrysostom

Marriage is an act of will that signifies and involves a mutual gift, which unites the spouses and binds them to their eventual souls, with whom they make up a sole family – a domestic church. Pope John Paul II

Motherhood Quotes

Finally brethren, whatever is true, whatever is honorable, whatever is just, whatever is pure, whatever is lovely, whatever is of a good report – if there is any virtue and if there is any praise – think on these things. Philippians 4:8

Her children rise up and call her blessed; Her husband also, and he praises her. Proverbs 31:2,8

Train up a child in the way he should go; even when he is old he will not depart from it. Proverbs 22:6

My son, keep your father's commandment, and forsake not your mother's teaching. Bind them on your heart always; tie them around your neck. When you walk, they will lead you; when you lie down, they will watch over you; and when you awake, they will talk with you. Proverbs 6:20-22

Honor your father and your mother, that your days may be long in the land that the Lord your God is giving you. Exodus 20:12

And let us not grow weary of doing good, for in due season we will reap, if we do not give up. Galatians 6:9

Only be careful, and watch yourselves closely so that you do not forget the things your eyes have seen or let them fade from your heart as long as you live. Teach them to your children and to their children after them. Deuteronomy 4:9

For I know the plans I have for you, declares the Lord, plans for peace and not for evil, to give you a future and a hope. Jeremiah 29:11

Surely goodness and mercy shall follow me all the days of my life, and I shall dwell in the house of the Lord forever. Psalm 23:6

Strength and dignity are her clothing, and she laughs at the time to come. She opens her mouth with wisdom, and the teaching of kindness is on her tongue. She looks well to the ways of her household and does not eat the bread of idleness. Her children rise up and call her blessed; her husband also, and he praises her: "Many women have done excellently, but you surpass them all." Charm is deceitful, and beauty is vain, but a woman who fears the LORD is to be praised. Give her of the fruit of her hands, and let her works praise her in the gates. Proverbs 31:25-31

Let us run to Mary, and, as her little children, cast ourselves into her arms with a perfect confidence. -Saint Francis de Sales

It is not the actual physical exertion that counts towards a one's progress, nor the nature of the task, but by the spirit of faith with which it is undertaken. -Saint Francis Xavier

Sanctify yourself and you will sanctify society. - Saint Francis of Assisi

If we wish to make any progress in the service of God we must begin every day of our life with new eagerness. We must keep ourselves in the presence of God as much as possible and have no other view or end in all our actions but the divine honor. - Saint Charles Borromeo

We must pray without ceasing, in every occurrence and employment of our lives - that prayer which is rather a habit of lifting up the heart to God as in a constant communication with Him. - Saint Elizabeth Ann Seton

Finances Quotes

For where your treasure is, there your heart will be also. Mathew 6:21

Bring the whole tithe into the storehouse, that there may be food in my house. Test me in this, "says the Lord Almighty, "and see if I will not throw open the floodgates of heaven and pour out so much blessing that there will not be room enough to store it. Malachi 3:10

Whoever loves money never has enough; whoever loves wealth is never satisfied with their income. This too is meaningless. Ecclesiastes 5:10

Dishonest money dwindles away, but whoever gathers money little by little makes it grow. Proverbs 13:11

Keep your lives free from the love of money and be content with what you have, because God has said, "Never will I leave you; never will I forsake you." Hebrews 13:5

No one can serve two masters. Either you will hate the one and love the other, or you will be devoted to the one and despise the other. You cannot serve both God and money. Matthew 6:24

For the love of money is the root of all kinds of evil. Some people, eager for money, have wandered from the faith and pierced themselves with many griefs. 1 Timothy 6:10

Command those who are rich in this present world not to be arrogant nor to put their hope in wealth, which is so uncertain, but to put their hope in God, who richly provides us with everything for our enjoyment. Command them to do good, to be rich in good deeds, and to be generous and willing to share. In this way they will lay up treasure for themselves as a firm foundation for the coming age, so that they may take hold of the life that is truly life. 1 Timothy 6:17-19

Lazy hands make for poverty, but diligent hands bring wealth. Proverbs 10:4

If you are attached to the things of this earth, you should give alms sufficient to enable you to punish your avarice by depriving yourself of all that is not absolutely necessary for life. - St. John Vianney

Rest Quotes

Then, because so many people were coming and going that they did not even have a chance to eat, he said to them, "Come with me by yourselves to a quiet place and get some rest. Mark 6:31

Rather, it should be that of your inner self, the unfading beauty of a gentle and quiet spirit, which is of great worth in God's sight. 1 Peter 3:4

But I have calmed and quieted myself, I am like a weaned child with its mother; like a weaned child I am content. Psalm 131:2

The fear of the Lord leads to life; then one rests content, untouched by trouble. Proverbs 19:23

So God blessed the seventh day and made it holy, because on it God rested from all his work that he had done in creation. Genesis 2:3

My presence will go with you, and I will give you rest. Exodus 33:14

Remember the Sabbath day, to keep it holy. Six days you shall labor, and do all your work, but the seven day is the Sabbath to the Lord your God. On it you shall not do any work, you or your son, or your daughter… Exodus 20:8-10

My soul finds rest in God alone; my salvation comes from him. He alone is my rock and my salvation; he is my fortress, I will never be shaken. Psalm 62:1-2

Let us therefore strive to enter that rest, so that no one may fall by the same sort of disobedience. Hebrews 4:9-11

Come to me, all you who are weary and burdened, and I will give you rest. Take my yoke upon you and learn from me, for I am gentle and humble in heart, and you will find rest for your souls. Matthew 11:28

Casting all your anxieties on him, because he cares for you. 1 Peter 5:7

These things I have spoken to you, that in Me you may have peace. In the world you have tribulation, but take courage; I have overcome the world. John 16:33

Yes, my soul, find rest in God: my hope comes from him. Psalm 62:5

But godliness with contentment is great gain. 1 Timothy 6:6

Be anxious for nothing, but in everything by prayer and supplication with thanksgiving let your requests be made known to God. And the peace of God, which surpasses all comprehension, shall guard your hearts and your minds in Christ Jesus. Philippians 4:6-7

Peace I leave with you; My peace I give to you; not as the world gives, do I give to you. Let not your heart be troubled, nor let it be fearful. John 14:27

Lay your head on my shoulder, rest and regain your strength. I am always with you. - Jesus to St. Faustina

Our hearts were made for you, O Lord, and they are restless until they rest in you. – St. Augustine of Hippo

Health Quotes

19 Do you not know that your bodies are temples of the Holy Spirit, who is in you, whom you have received from God? You are not your own; 20 you were bought at a price. Therefore honor God with your bodies. 1 Corinthians 6:19-20

31 So whether you eat or drink or whatever you do, do it all for the glory of God. I Corinthians 10:31

8 For physical training is of some value, but godliness has value for all things, holding promise for both the present life and the life to come. 1 Timothy 4:8

22 A cheerful heart is good medicine, but a crushed spirit dries up the bones. Proverbs 17:22

17 She sets about her work vigorously; her arms are strong for her tasks. Proverbs 31:17

18 Do not get drunk on wine, which leads to debauchery. Instead, be filled with the Spirit. Ephesians 5:18

24 Gracious words are a honeycomb, sweet to the soul and healing to the bones. Proverbs 16:24

7 Do not be wise in your own eyes; fear the LORD and shun evil. 8 This will bring health to your body and nourishment to your bones. Proverbs 3:7-8

It is not the soul alone that should be healthy; if the mind is healthy in a healthy body, all will be healthy and much better prepared to give God greater service. – St. Ignatius of Loyola

Concerning the harsh treatment of the body for our Lord's sake, I would say, avoid anything that would cause the shedding even of a drop of blood. – St. Ignatius of Loyola

It is so natural for people to seek pleasure in eating and drinking that Saint Paul, teaching early Christians to perform all their actions for the love and glory of God, is obliged to mention eating and drinking specifically, for it is difficult to eat without offending God. Most people eat like animals to satisfy their appetite. – St. Jean-Baptiste de la Salle

If you have promised Christ to go by the straight and narrow way, restrain your stomach, because by pleasing and enlarging it, you break your contract. Attend and you will hear Him who says: "Spacious and broad is the way of the belly that leads to the perdition of fornication, and many there are who go in by it; because narrow is the gate and strait is the way of fasting that leads to the life of purity, and few there be that find it. – St. John Climacus

As long as the vice of gluttony has a hold on a man, all that he has done valiantly is forfeited by him: and as long as the belly is unrestrained, all virtue comes to naught. – Pope St. Gregory the Great

Homemaking Quotes

In all toil there is profit, but mere talk tends only to poverty. Proverbs 14:23

For God is not unjust so as to overlook your work and the love that you have shown for his name in serving the saints, as you still do. Hebrews 6:10

Whatever you do, work heartily, as for the Lord and not for men. Colossians 3:23

Do not be anxious about anything, but in everything by prayer and supplication with thanksgiving let your requests be made known to God. Philippians 4:6

Whoever is slack in his work is a brother to him who destroys. Proverbs 18:9

Casting all your anxieties on him, because he cares for you. 1 Peter 5:7

So flee youthful passions and pursue righteousness, faith, love, and peace, along with those who call on the Lord from a pure heart. 2 Timothy 2:22

And to aspire to live quietly, and to mind your own affairs, and to work with your hands, as we instructed you. 1 Thessalonians 4:11

Let the word of Christ dwell in you richly, teaching and admonishing one another in all wisdom, singing psalms and hymns and spiritual songs, with thankfulness in your hearts to God. Colossians 3:16

The most important work you will ever do will be within the walls of your own home. - President Harold Be Lee.

Homemaking is surely in reality the most important work in the world. - C. S. Lewis

You can't just buy an apartment and furnish it and walk away. It's the flowers you choose, the music you play, the smile you have waiting. I want it to be gay and cheerful, a haven in this troubled world. I don't want my husband and my children to come home and find a rattled woman. Our era is already rattled enough, isn't it? - Audrey Hepburn

Have regular hours for work and play, make each day both useful and pleasant, and prove that you understand the worth of time by employing it well. - Louisa May Alcott

I am still determined to be cheerful and happy in whatsoever circumstance I may be; for I have also learnt from experience that the greater part of our happiness or misery depends upon our dispositions and not upon our circumstances. - Martha Washington

Thus the little domestic Church, like the greater Church, needs to be constantly and intensely evangelized: hence its duty regarding permanent education in the faith...the family, like the Church, ought to be a place where the Gospel is transmitted and from which the Gospel radiates...the future of evangelization depends in great part on the Church of the home. - Pope John Paul II

End Notes

[1] "eHarmony," 12 Sept. 2016 <http://www.eharmony.com>.

[2] As Fr. John Riccardo says often, "Love begins when the feelings are gone."

[3] "Quotes From the Saints 2," 12 Sept. 2016 <http://www.catholicBible101.com/quotesfromthesaints2.htm>.

[4] "Mary Faustina Kowalska Quotes and Sayings," 12 Sept. 2016 <http://www.inspiringquotes.us/author/8949-mary-faustina-kowalska>.

[5] Saint Louis de Montfort, The Secret of the Rosary (Tan Books & Publisher, 1976).

[6] Fr. Michael Gaitley, 33 Days To Morning Glory (Marian Press, 2011).

[7] Saint Louis de Montfort, True Devotion (Monfort Pubns, 1984).

[8] Fr. Michael Gaitley, 33 Days To Morning Glory (Marian Press, 2011) PG 139.

[9] "Saints' Quotes," 12 Sept. 2016 < http://saintsquotes.net/selection%20-%20fewness.html>.

[10] Anthony DeStefano Travel Guide To Heaven (Image, 2005).

[11] Songs Kids Love To Sing, 25 Sunday School Song,s Straightway Music, 2003.

[12] Jeff Cavins, When You Suffer: Biblical Keys for Hope and Understanding (Severant Books, 2015).

[13] Marguerite Duportals, How To Make Sense of Suffering (Sophia Institute Press, 2013).

[14] Jeannie Ewing, From Grief to Grace (Sophia Institute Press, 2016).

[15] Gregory Popcak, For Better…Forever (Our Sunday Visitor, 2015).

[16] Emerson Eggerichs, Love and Respect (Thomas Nelson, 2004).

[17] Gary Chapman, The 5 Love Languages (Northfield Publishing, 2015).

[18] Art and Loraine Bennett The Temperament God Gave Your Spouse (Sophia Institute Press, 2008).

[19] "16 Personalities," 12 Sept. 2016 <http://www.16personalities.com>.

[20] Sterling Jaquith, "Communication Breakdown," 12 Sept. 2016 < http://sterlingjaquith.com/communication-breakdown/>.

[21] "Discover Your Love Language," 12 Sept. 2016 <http://www.5lovelanguages.com/profile/>.

[22] Michael Hyatt and Daniel Karkavy, Living Forward (Baker Books, 2016). PG 16.

23 "We Choose Virtues," 12 Sept. 2016 <https://www.romancatholicman.com/70-saints-quotes-to-elevate-your-game/>.

24 Holly Pierlot, A Mother's Rule of Life: How to Bring Order to Your Home and Peace to Your Soul (Sophia Institute Press, 2004).

25 Holly Pierlot, A Mother's Rule of Life: How to Bring Order to Your Home and Peace to Your Soul (Sophia Institute Press, 2004).

26 "Quotes by Saints," 12 Sept. 2016 <http://www.bostoncatholic.org/Being-Catholic/Content.aspx?id=11480>.

27 S.O.L.T. Miriam James Heidland, Loved As I Am: An Invitaiton to Conersion, Healing, and Freedom through Jesus (Ave Maria Press, 2014).

28 Brian Johnson, "Optimize Your Life with Brian Johnson," 12 Sept. 2016 <https://brianjohnson.me/>.

29 Dave Ramsey, "Financial Peace University." 12 Sept. 2016 <http://www.daveramsey.com/store/financial-peace-university/financial-peace-university-membership-all-new/prod614.html?ectid=gaw.fpu-general2>.

30 Dave Ramsey, The Total Money Makeover: A Proven Plan For Success (Thomas Nelson, 2013).

31 Joshua Becker, Clutter Free with Kids (Becoming Minimalist, 2014).

32 "FODMAP Food List," 12 Sept. 2016 <http://www.ibsdiets.org/fodmap-diet/fodmap-food-list/>.

33 Katie Warner, Head and Heart: Becoming Spiritual Leaders for Your Family (Emmaus Road Publishing, 2015).

34 Sarah Mackenzie, "Amongst Lovely Things," 12 Sept. 2016 <http://www.amongstlovelythings.com/>.

35 Sterling Jaquith, "Catholic Mom Challenge Facebook Group," 12 Sept. 2016 <https://www.facebook.com/groups/catholicmomchallenge>.

36 Scott Adams, How to Fail at Almost Everything and Still Win Big: Kind of the Story of My Life (Portfolio, 2014).

37 Scott Adams, How to Fail at Almost Everything and Still Win Big: Kind of the Story of My Life (Portfolio, 2014).

38 Sherry Weddell, Forming Intentional Disciples: The Path to Knowing and Following Jesus (Our Sunday Visitor, 2012).

39 "Saint Augustine Quotes," 12 Sept. 2016 <http://www.brainyquote.com/quotes/quotes/s/saintaugus165165.html>.

40 "G.K. Chesterton Quotes," 12 Sept. 2016 <https://www.goodreads.com/quotes/127319-the-most-extraordinary-

thing-in-the-world-is-an-ordinary>.

[41] Fr. Michael Gaitley, <u>33 Days To Morning Glory</u> (Marian Press, 2011) PG 33.

[42] "70 Saint Quotes to Elevate Your Game!," 12 Sept. 2016 <https://www.romancatholicman.com/70-saints-quotes-to-elevate-your-game/>.

[43] "Pope John Paul II Quotes," 12 Sept. 2016 <http://www.brainyquote.com/quotes/quotes/p/popejohnpa178860.html>.

[44] "S.M.A.R.T. Criteria" 12 Sept. 2016 <https://en.wikipedia.org/wiki/SMART_criteria>.

[45] C.S. Lewis, <u>The Screwtape Letters</u> (HarperOne, 2015).

[4646] Hallie Lord, <u>On The Other Side of Fear: How I Found Peace</u> (Our Sunday Visitor, 2016)

[47] Brian Johnson "Optimal Living 101 Master Classes," 12 Sept. 2016 <https://brianjohnson.me/master-classes/>.

[48] Piers Steel, <u>The Procrastination Equation: How to Stop Putting Things Off and Start Getting Things Done</u> (Harper Perennial, 2012).

[49] Brian Johnson "Optimal Living 101 Master Classes," 12 Sept. 2016 <https://brianjohnson.me/master-classes/>.

[50] "Edith Stein Quotes," 12 Sept. 2016 < http://ocarm.org/en/content/ocarm/edith-stein-quotes>.

[51] Deacon Dr. Bob McDonald, "Anger and Forgiveness," 12 Sept. 2016 <https://www.lighthousecatholicmedia.org/store/title/anger-and-forgiveness>.

[52] Brian Johnson "Optimal Living 101 Master Classes," 12 Sept. 2016 <https://brianjohnson.me/master-classes/>.

[53] Katie Warner, <u>Head and Heart: Becoming Spiritual Leaders for Your Family</u> (Emmaus Road Publishing, 2015).

[54] VidAngel, 12 Sept. 2016 http://www.vidangel.com.

[55] Brian Johnson "Optimal Living 101 Master Classes," 12 Sept. 2016 <https://brianjohnson.me/master-classes/>.

[56] Brian Johnson "Optimal Living 101 Master Classes," 12 Sept. 2016 <https://brianjohnson.me/master-classes/>.

[57] Darren Hardy, <u>The Compound Effect</u> (Vanguard Press, 2012).

[58] Brian Johnson "Optimal Living 101 Master Classes," 12 Sept. 2016 <https://brianjohnson.me/master-classes/>.

[59] Brian Johnson "Optimal Living 101 Master Classes," 12 Sept. 2016 <https://brianjohnson.me/master-classes/>.

[60] Brian Johnson "Optimal Living 101 Master Classes," 12 Sept. 2016 <https://brianjohnson.me/master-classes/>.

[61] Brian Johnson "Optimal Living 101 Master Classes," 12 Sept. 2016 <https://brianjohnson.me/master-classes/>.

[62] Fr. Larry Richards, Be A Man (Ignatius Press, 2009).

[63] Raylan J Alleman, Catholic Manhood Today (CreateSpace Independent Publishing Platform, 2016)

[64] Luke 10:38-42.

[65] "Pareto Analysis," 12 Sept. 2016 <https://en.wikipedia.org/wiki/Time_management#Pareto_analysis>.

[66] "Covey Matrix," 12 Sept. 2016 https://commons.wikimedia.org/wiki/File:MerrillCoveyMatrix.png

[67] Hallie Lord, On The Other Side of Fear: How I Found Peace (Our Sunday Visitor, 2016)

[68] "Elizabeth Elliot Quotes," 12 Sept. 2016 <https://www.goodreads.com/quotes/915294-don-t-dig-up-in-doubt-what-you-planted-in-faith>.

[69] "Bright Line Eating" 12 Sept. 2016 <http://susanpeircethompson.com/bright-line-eating/>.

[70] "Bright Line Eating" 12 Sept. 2016 <http://susanpeircethompson.com/bright-line-eating/>.

[71] "Humility," 12 Sept. 2016 <http://whitelilyoftrinity.com/saints_quotes_humility.html>.

About The Author

Sterling Jaquith lives in Boise, Idaho with her husband, their three young daughters, and a lazy border collie. She has a degree in finance from Seattle University and is a certified dog trainer. She blogs at www.sterlingjaquith.com and her podcast Coffee & Pearls comes out on Tuesdays.

Her husband Michael has a podcast, The Catholic Commute, that comes out on Mondays and Wednesdays designed for men to listen to on their way to work! You can read more about his projects at www.thestakesarehigh.com.

Sterling loves speaking at conferences and retreats, sharing her conversion story and the message that we should all be striving for sainthood! You can read more of her writings at www.catholicmom.com and www.catholic365.com